HR MIRROR 500

BEYOND DASHBOARD, STORIES HR IS MISSING

PRARTHANA KARMAKAR,
ABHINANDAN MOOKHERJEE

Clever Fox®
PUBLISHING

CLEVER FOX PUBLISHING
Chennai, India

Published by CLEVER FOX PUBLISHING 2025

ISBN: 978-93-7500-417-2

CONTENTS

ACKNOWLEDGEMENTS

This work is the outcome of collective effort, insight, and encouragement.

We, **Prarthana Karmakar** and **Abhinandan Mookherjee**, wish to express our sincere gratitude to **Ms Gargi Nath, Program Manager at TalentSynergy**, for her valuable contribution in shaping the initial visualization of the cover photo. Her creative input played a crucial role in giving this project its initial visual identity.

We also acknowledge the contributions of the **FresherRank internship Program**, whose thoughtful conversations and support, though brief, provided diverse perspectives that enriched our approach to this work.

Finally, we extend our heartfelt thanks to all colleagues, mentors, and well-wishers who have supported and inspired us throughout this journey.

THE HR ANALYTICS HANDBOOK: PREFACE

In today's data-fueled world, while enterprises mature from automated to autonomous, the people function organization and HR are undergoing a profound transformation. Despite the rapid growth of digital HR tools, dashboards, and AI platforms, most organizations still wrestle with a fundamental question: *"What do we truly know about our people?" while the demand is to deploy machines that learn, reason, and act*—not just humans making decisions from data.

The HR Analytics Handbook series is conceptualized to address a core fundamental point to support this journey. Drawing on a foundation of statistical thinking and decades of professional practice, this multi-volume series bridges the gap between raw data and business decisions. Unlike technical manuals or purely academic works, it takes a practitioner-first approach - combining rigor with real-world HR approaches.

Each volume focuses deeply on one HR theme Headcount, Engagement, Performance, Pay, and Attrition-mapping business questions to metrics, data structures & key reports, visualizations to carve out decision-making frameworks. By breaking the business problems into multiple volumes, the series enables readers to develop expertise step by step, building a solid foundation across the different domains of HR analytics.

The intended audience is wide: Ranging from HR Practitioners implementing the HR analytics framework in organizations, HR leaders seeking better insights, business managers aiming to impact people practices, and aspiring analysts eager to connect data with stories and strategy.

Whether you are owning up the reporting function, interpreting dashboards, conducting workforce modeling, or designing employee engagement/rewards & growth/retention programs, this series equips you to fast-track the base-work in building a matured people analytics framework, that enables the people organization to move beyond descriptive (traditional) reporting towards identifying critical people impact areas through a diagnostic predictive/prescriptive approach.

Volume 1: Theme 'Headcount' opens with the most fundamental dimension of people analytics—understanding *who* makes up the workforce. From there, the series progresses into increasingly complex and strategic areas, creating a comprehensive roadmap for mastering HR analytics in practice.

In Essence:

The HR Mirror 500 (HR Analytics Handbook) is conceptualized as a multi-volume series that bridges the gap between HR data and business decisions. Written with a practitioner-first approach, each volume explores each of the people impact areas – Headcount (this volume), Engagement, Performance, Pay, and Attrition (Volumes 2 to 5) - linking business questions to metrics, data models, and decision paths. The series is designed for HR leaders, managers, and analysts who want to turn numbers into strategic insights.

HOW TO GET THE MOST FROM THIS BOOK

Your Guide to the "Headcount" Journey

This book is built for action. We move beyond theory, using realistic stories and diagnostic questions to help you see your own organization in a new light. While company names have been changed, each scenario represents a common challenge faced by modern enterprises, making the insights directly relatable and applicable.

The chapters within this volume follow a logical, sequential narrative:

- **We start with the Foundation (Chapters 1-3):** First, we understand the current state of your workforce—its **Composition, Demographics, & Structure**. Then, we look forward with **Workforce Planning & Forecasting** to anticipate future needs, which naturally leads to analyzing **Skill Trends & Gaps** to bridge where you are and where you need to be.
- **We then explore Talent Dynamics (Chapters 4-7):** Next, we examine how talent moves and grows within your organization through **Internal Movement, Promotions & Career Paths,** and how work is organized via **Job Structure, Shifts & Scheduling**. We then look at how talent enters through **Hiring, Sourcing & Pipeline,** and how it exits or is retained in **Internal Movement and Attrition**.
- **We conclude with the Employee Lifecycle (Chapters 8-9):** Finally, we focus on key moments that define the employee experience and its impact on stability, covering **Onboarding, Tenure, and Experience,** and the critical link between **Onboarding, Attrition, and Experience**.

A Consistent Blueprint for Insight

Every chapter in this volume is structured with a clear, repeatable framework to maximize your learning

Business Context
We set the stage. Why is this topic a strategic lever for the business?

Relevant Data Sources
We get practical. Where can you find the necessary data in your systems?

Stories from the Front Lines
We bring it to life. Real-world scenarios show you how companies have successfully diagnosed and solved problems.

The Essential Questions
We equip you for action. A curated list of strategic questions to spark your own analysis and leadership discussions.

Key Takeaways
We distill the insights. A concise summary of the chapter's most critical lessons.

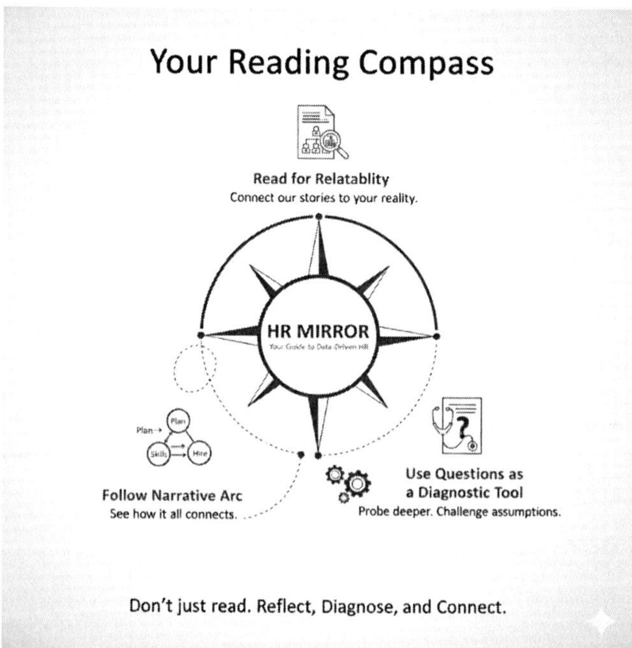

CHAPTER 1

WORKFORCE COMPOSITION, DEMOGRAPHICS & STRUCTURE

Section 1: Introduction

Workforce composition is where each HR analytics journey begins. Think of it as taking a snapshot of your organization's people—who they are, how they are distributed across different roles, functions, and locations. It's not just about headcount; it's about understanding the story behind those numbers.

Why does this matter? It matters because the diversity of your workforce directly influences how ready your organization is to deliver, grow, adapt, and sustain the core business delivery aspects. For example, if most of the junior hires are freshers, that signals a bigger investment in training and onboarding, including cultural assimilation. If gender diversity is skewed towards a specific gender across levels, especially in leadership roles, it raises questions about career progression, succession planning, and an equal opportunity employer. Additionally, regions showing a sharp spike in hiring reveal the growth market focus for the organization.

These patterns aren't just interesting—they're strategic. While the number of employees nearing retirement exposes future knowledge gaps, departments overloaded with too many people doing overtime may struggle with flexibility & health issues. A lack of academic diversity might limit innovation and problem-solving. With the right analysis, HR leaders can spot risks early and make targeted decisions that strengthen the organization's capability.

Workforce composition is more than a headcount exercise—it's the first lens through which equity, balance, and readiness are revealed. For a CHRO, one critical metric is **"diverse representation in leadership roles"** because it directly impacts both business resilience and external reputation. Tracking gender, age, and cultural diversity across leadership not only exposes structural gaps but also signals whether the organization is living its values.

At the heart of it all lies one deceptively simple question: **"What talent comprises the workforce today?"** This chapter helps you answer that with clarity. Together, we'll explore the essential business questions, the right data sources, and the visual storytelling techniques that bring workforce insights to life—so you can move from data to action with confidence.

Section 2: Data Sources

Prior to analyzing the workforce composition, we need to know *where the data comes from*. Think of it like putting together a jigsaw puzzle—you need all the right pieces before the picture makes sense. In HR, those pieces usually come from four main sources:

1. Primary System of record: Human Resource Information System (HRIS)

This is the organization's "master record" for people data. It stores all details like job roles, departments, grades, locations, hire dates, tenure, reporting lines, and demographics such as age and gender. If you've ever seen charts on headcount, gender ratios, or age mix in the workforce, that's HRIS data in action.

☞ *Example:* If you want to see how many employees are under 30, or check the gender split in sales vs. finance, HRIS is where you would find the base info.

2. Systems of transaction: Talent Lifecycle Systems

These act as transaction systems capturing each step of the employee journey. Onboarding records hires and readiness, learning tracks courses and certifications, performance captures reviews and ratings, compensation manages pay and rewards, and succession logs pipeline moves. Together, they form the transaction backbone of how employees enter, grow, get paid, perform, progress & exit.

☞ *Example:* Want to know the new joiner pipeline, the systems of reference are the ATS and Onboarding system, whether most of your hires studied engineering, commerce, or arts? That's what the ATS can show you.

3. Engagement, Sentiment & Experience Insights:

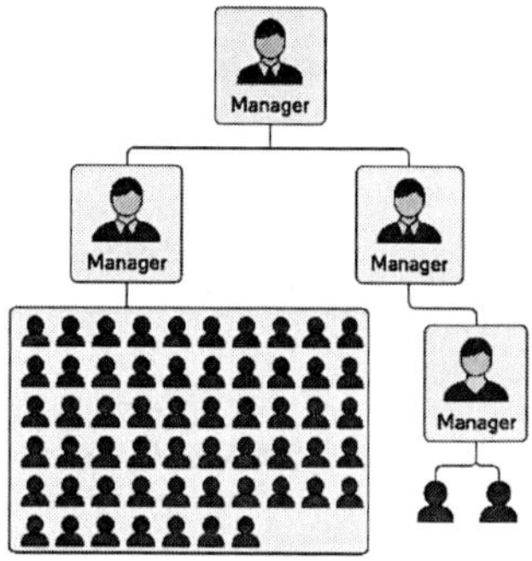

Engagement surveys, feedback tools, recognition platforms, and wellbeing apps measure how employees **feel about their work and culture**. This layer provides critical context beyond transactions — sentiment and experience.

☞ *Example:* For instance, pulse survey results may show that **frontline teams score 10 points lower in eNPS** compared to corporate employees, which signals the need for targeted manager enablement or communication interventions.

4. Offline & External / Unstructured Data Sources:

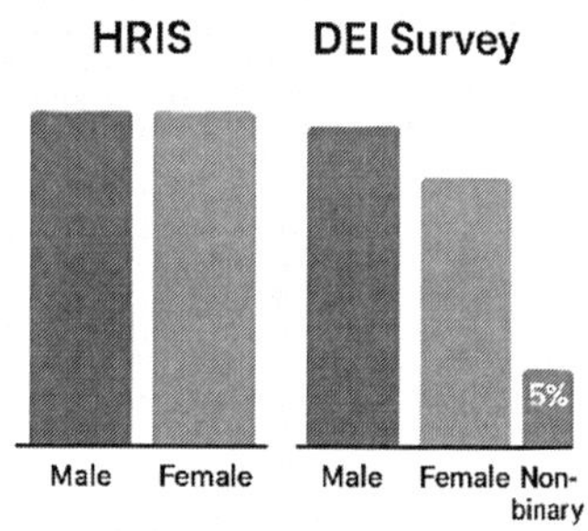

Not all insights come from structured systems — a lot emerges through **coffee chats, watercooler conversations, power lunches, and townhall questions** where employees voice concerns or share ideas informally. Managers may also maintain spreadsheets, ad hoc trackers, or offline notes that capture context not found in core systems. External inputs such as compensation surveys, ESG benchmarks, or compliance/client audit findings add further perspective.

☞ *Example:* For example, an internal audit might flag manual overtime tracking at one plant, while townhall feedback highlights fairness concerns, together prompting leadership to automate rostering and ensure global labor law compliance.

When these pieces are combined, we move from scattered records to a clear, trustworthy view of the organization. The magic isn't just in collecting data—it's in connecting it across all these areas, for CXOs & leaders can see the workforce story unfold in real time.

Section 3: The Composition Mirror – Building a Resilient, Not Just Large, Workforce

The Illusion of Strength: When Headcount Hides Systemic Weakness

GlobalSynergy, a multinational enterprise with 7,000 employees, presented a picture of robust health. Its annual reports showcased a steadily climbing headcount, new offices sprouting across the globe, and a narrative of unstoppable growth. To the board and the market, the company was a talent magnet, successfully scaling to meet demand. But this top-line number, the celebrated headcount, was a facade. It concealed deep, structural fissures that were quietly eroding the company's innovation, stability, and long-term viability. The true story of GlobalSynergy wasn't in the number of people it employed, but in the composition of that population—a story of imbalance, missed opportunity, and unmanaged risk.

The Homogeneous Pipeline: When Pedigree Trumps Potential

The first crack in the foundation appeared in the company's hiring halls. For years, GlobalSynergy had prided itself on recruiting from a small cluster of "target" universities—esteemed institutions that reliably produced high-achieving graduates. On the surface, this was an efficient, quality-assuring strategy. But a deeper analysis revealed a critical lack of cognitive diversity. The company was filled with people who thought in the same ways, approached problems with similar methodologies, and had nearly identical academic pedigrees. This homogeneity was stifling innovation. When faced with disruptive market challenges, their teams struggled to generate the novel, out-of-the-box thinking required to compete.

This critical blind spot was exposed by a fundamental question about talent sourcing:

1. Are we hiring talent from a diverse range of academic backgrounds? – This moves beyond prestige to probe the variety of thought and problem-solving approaches in your workforce. A narrow academic pipeline, as GlobalSynergy discovered, risks creating an echo chamber, limiting the innovative capacity necessary for long-term survival.

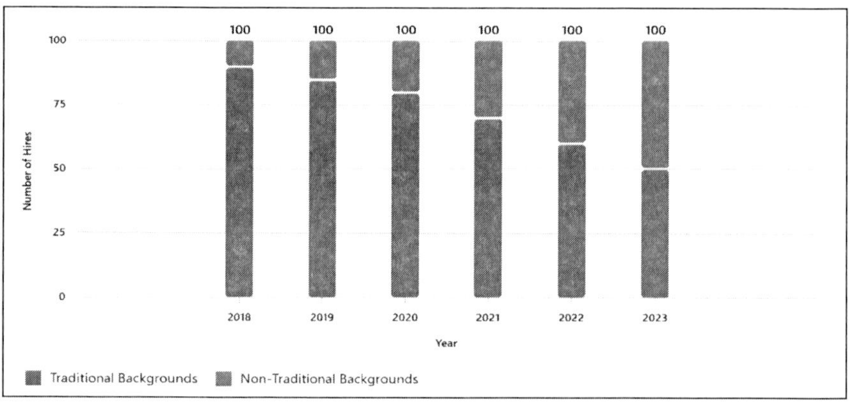

Graph 1.1: Broadening the Talent Pipeline: GlobalSynergy's Shift Toward Diverse Academic Backgrounds

The solution was not to abandon elite schools, but to broaden the aperture. GlobalSynergy's talent acquisition team began actively building relationships with state universities, technical colleges, and coding bootcamps. They launched an "Alternative Pathways" internship, specifically seeking candidates with non-traditional educational backgrounds. The result was an infusion of new perspectives that began to challenge entrenched assumptions and spark more creative solutions.

The Experience Chasm: The Peril of a Lopsided Workforce

Simultaneously, a dangerous imbalance was brewing in the experience level of the workforce. In a well-intentioned but short-sighted effort to control labor costs, leadership had mandated a hiring freeze on mid- and senior-level roles while aggressively recruiting entry-level graduates. The strategy delivered immediate salary savings, but the long-term cost was catastrophic.

Managers, who were once team leaders, found themselves acting as full-time trainers, their own productivity plummeting as they scrambled to onboard waves of inexperienced hires. Client satisfaction scores nosedived as "rookie mistakes" multiplied—from misconfigured software deployments to poorly handled customer inquiries. The organization had become top-heavy with leaders and bottom-heavy with learners, with a cavernous gap in the middle where the experienced "doers" should have been.

This operational crisis was precipitated by ignoring a couple of crucial strategic questions:

2. Are new hires more likely to be experienced or entry level?
   – This shows whether the company is investing in fresh potential, seasoned expertise, or, critically, a healthy balance of both. GlobalSynergy's lopsided approach created a capability vacuum that directly threatened service quality and client trust.
3. Which functions have the highest filler/turnover rates for entry-level positions?
   – This question is a direct and vital follow-up to point to the specific functions (e.g., Customer Support, Junior Analyst roles) where the aggressive entry-level hiring strategy is failing, leading to a costly "revolving door." Analyzing this data would reveal whether the "rookie mistakes" and client dissatisfaction are concentrated

in specific departments, allowing for targeted interventions in onboarding, management, or role design to improve retention.

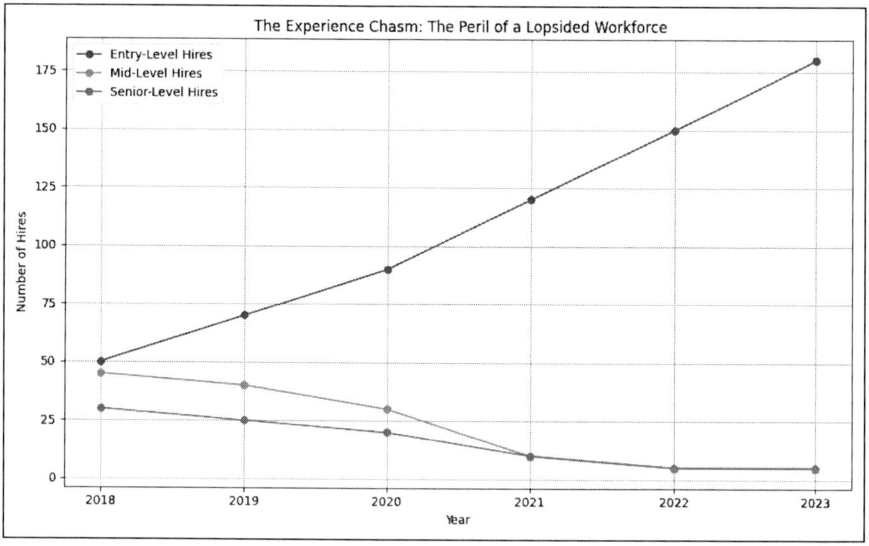

Graph 1.2: The Experience Chasm: The Peril of a Lopsided Workforce

To rebalance the ship, HR had to make a compelling case to reverse the hiring freeze on experienced professionals. They implemented a "Blended Team" model, ensuring that every project team had a mix of entry-level, mid-career, and senior talent. This not only stabilized performance but also created a natural mentoring environment, accelerating the development of their junior hires in a way that formal training never could.

The Frozen Middle: When Diversity is a Mirage

GlobalSynergy's public commitment to diversity was unwavering. Company-wide, women constituted a respectable 40% of the workforce. However, this aggregate number was a masterclass in masking the truth. A level-by-level analysis revealed a deeply troubling trend: while women were well-represented in entry and junior-level roles, their presence sharply declined at each successive rung of the corporate ladder. By the time it reached the senior leadership team, female representation had plummeted to a mere 15%.

This was not a pipeline problem; it was a promotion problem. High-potential junior women looked up, saw no one who looked like them in the seats of power, and logically concluded that a ceiling existed. This perception became a self-fulfilling prophecy, leading to a higher attrition rate among talented women at the mid-career stage—precisely the point where they should have been stepping into leadership.

This hidden equity crisis was uncovered by asking two diagnostic questions in tandem:

4. What is the diversity split at the organization level?
   – This highlights whether representation is truly balanced or merely an illusion created by aggregating data. It forces the organization to look at the distribution of power and opportunity, not just overall numbers.
5. What is the breakdown of our workforce by business unit, level, and gender?
   – This is the foundational data question that exposes the "frozen middle" phenomenon described in the text. It moves beyond the aggregate number (40% women) to reveal the specific business units and job levels where women are underrepresented, directly illustrating the "promotion problem" and the attrition of mid-career women.
6. Where do we observe gender imbalance within business units or job levels?
   – This is the actionable, diagnostic follow-up to the breakdown. Once the data shows a decline in female representation at senior levels, this question forces a deeper dive into which specific business units (e.g., Engineering, Sales) or job levels (e.g., Director, Vice

President) are the primary contributors to the overall imbalance, allowing for targeted solutions like the sponsorship programs mentioned.

7. Are more women moving into senior management positions year over year?
– This tracks the flow of talent into leadership, measuring the effectiveness of inclusion efforts beyond mere hiring. For years, GlobalSynergy's answer was "no," revealing a stagnant system.

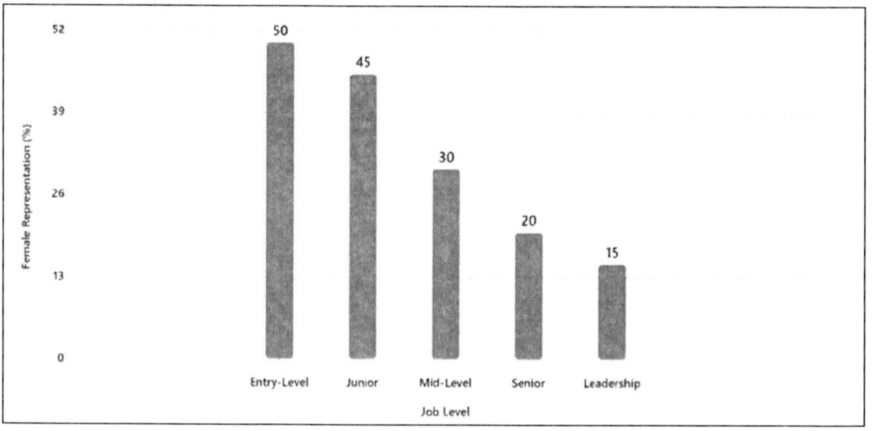

Graph 1.3: The Frozen Middle: When Diversity is a Mirage

The response had to be systemic. GlobalSynergy moved beyond generic diversity training. They implemented structured mentorship and, more importantly, sponsorship programs, where senior leaders were explicitly tasked with advocating for high-potential women. They introduced transparent promotion criteria and audited promotion decisions for gender bias. It was a slow, deliberate process, but over time, the logjam began to break, and the leadership team started to reflect the diversity of the wider workforce.

The Demographic Cliff: Navigating Generational Seas

A comprehensive age audit delivered the next shock. The workforce was overwhelmingly young, with nearly half of all employees under the age of 30. This created a dynamic, digitally-native culture, but it also meant a profound shortage of institutional memory and seasoned judgment. Clients began to comment on the lack of "grey-haired wisdom" on their account teams.

Even more alarming, deep within specific functions like manufacturing and operations, HR identified pockets that were the mirror opposite: teams heavily populated with employees aged 55 and above. These were repositories of irreplaceable, tacit knowledge—the veteran engineer who knew the secret to calibrating a legacy machine, the operations manager who navigated a supply chain crisis every decade. The company was five years away from a mass exodus of this critical expertise.

This dual risk—of inexperience and impending brain drain—was flagged by probing demographic questions:

8. What is the age breakdown of our current workforce?
   – This provides a sense of the generational mix, revealing whether the organization is positioned for long-term sustainability or facing a future dominated by inexperience.
9. Are there any teams/pockets within the organization that are heavily skewed toward nearing-retirement employees?
   – This identifies specific, high-risk areas where knowledge transfer is not just beneficial but urgent for business continuity.

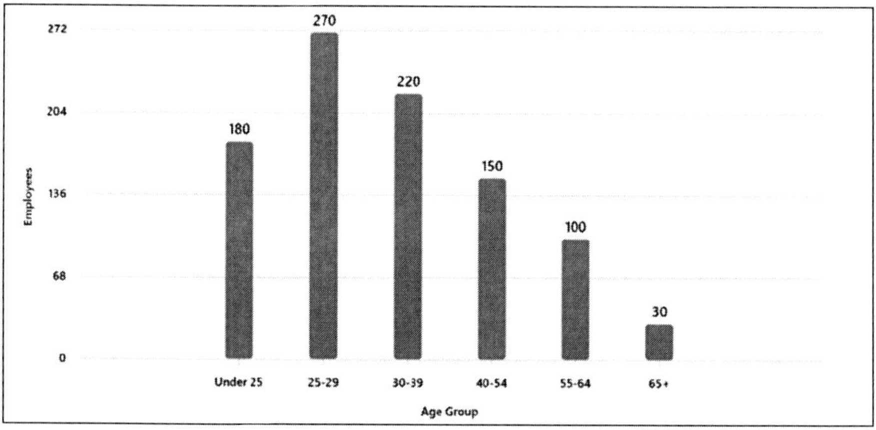

Graph 1.4: The Demographic Cliff: Navigating Generational Seas

The strategy was two-fold. For the young workforce, GlobalSynergy created "Reverse Mentoring" programs, where junior employees coached executives on digital trends, fostering mutual respect. For the retirement-risk teams, they launched a formal "Knowledge Harvesting" initiative, pairing veterans with successors to document processes and stories, turning individual knowledge into a collective asset.

The Bottleneck of Sameness: Role Concentration and Its Consequences

The structure of work itself came under scrutiny. An analysis of job roles within business units revealed severe concentrations. In the IT division, there was a glut of backend developers but a critical shortage of DevOps engineers and UX/UI designers. This meant that projects would consistently bottleneck—code was written, but it couldn't be efficiently deployed or made user-friendly. Similarly, the R&D department was a kingdom of PhD scientists but lacked the product managers and data analysts needed to translate brilliant discoveries into viable commercial products.

These operational bottlenecks were identified by examining team construction:

10. Which departments have the highest job role concentration?
    – This identifies where talent is over-clustered in similar functions, creating inflexibility and single points of failure that can stall entire value streams.
11. Which business units have the most balanced mix of job roles?
    – This highlights teams that are structured for versatility and resilience, serving as a model for the rest of the organization.
12. Which location contains the greatest variety of job roles?
    – This question fits seamlessly here. While the section identifies that the IT division lacks DevOps engineers and R&D lacks product managers, this question would expand the analysis geographically. It would reveal whether the company's headquarters acts as a centralized hub for diverse functions or if certain satellite offices have developed a balanced, self-sufficient mix of roles. The answer would inform the "decentralization and development" plan, highlighting which locations are already models of versatility.

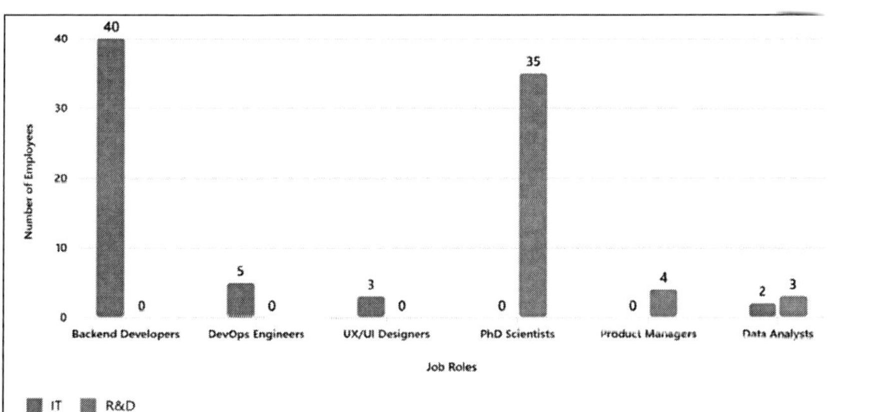

Graph 1.5: The Bottleneck of Sameness: Role Concentration and Its Consequences

Guided by this data, recruitment priorities were completely overhauled. Hiring plans were rewritten to target the missing roles, and internal mobility was encouraged to help rebalance the existing workforce. They moved to a product-based, cross-functional team model, forcing collaboration between previously siloed specialists and generalists.

The Geography of Opportunity: Location as a Determinant of Destiny

Finally, the physical distribution of the workforce told a powerful story about equity and risk. A geographic analysis showed that 60% of the company's employees were concentrated in one coastal megacity, making the business profoundly vulnerable to a localized disaster, as nearly happened during a season of floods. Furthermore, a map of gender distribution revealed stark contrasts: the headquarters was reasonably balanced, but a key engineering satellite office was over 90% male, undermining the company's stated diversity values.

Simultaneously, while headcount was exploding in lower-cost Tier-2 cities, support structures there were weak. Employees in these "growth hubs" felt like second-class citizens, with less access to HR, IT, and senior leadership, leading to higher localized attrition.

These geographic disparities were mapped using key distribution questions:

13. Which geographical region employs the most staff?
    – This shows where the company's operational core resides, revealing concentrations of risk.
14. How is our workforce distributed by location and gender?
    – This reveals whether inclusion is a company-wide reality or a headquarters-centric myth.

15. Where are our fastest-growing headcount locations?
    – This highlights regions requiring rapid investment in infrastructure and support to retain talent and ensure equitable employee experience.

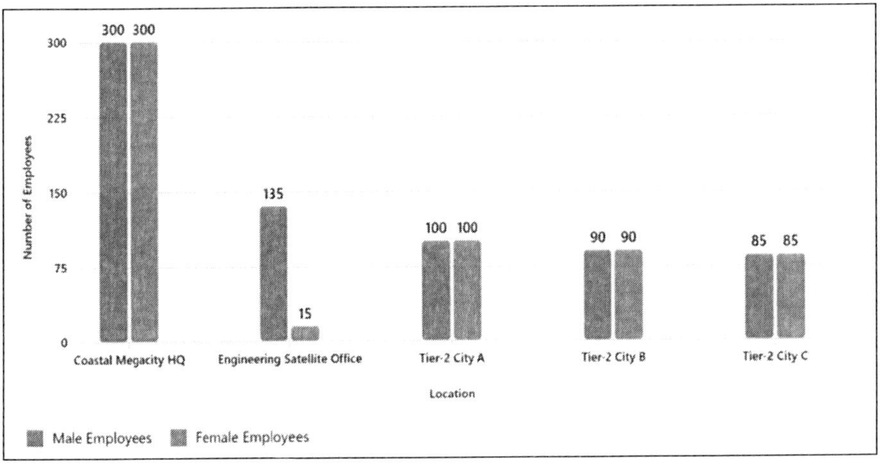

Graph 1.6: The Geography of Opportunity: Location as a Determinant of Destiny

The strategic response was a deliberate "decentralization and development" plan. Leadership is committed to building more robust HR and IT functions in the Tier-2 hubs. They launched location-specific diversity hiring campaigns and created a formalized remote work and job rotation policy to give employees in smaller offices access to the career-building opportunities previously reserved for headquarters staff.

The Transformation: From Counting Heads to Building Capability

The journey for GlobalSynergy was a profound paradigm shift. They learned that workforce data is not about passive counting; it is about active diagnosis. Every ignored imbalance—in background, experience, gender, age, role, or location—translated into a tangible business risk:

missed innovation, operational fragility, client dissatisfaction, and cultural erosion.

By systematically asking the fifteen essential questions about workforce composition, they moved from being proud of their size to being strategic about their shape. They stopped being a company that simply hired people and started being an organization that intentionally built a resilient, adaptable, and equitable human system. The headcount number remained important, but it was now understood as the starting point for a conversation, not the conclusion. In the end, GlobalSynergy didn't just have more employees; it had a better, stronger, and more future-ready workforce.

Section 4: Key Takeaways

So, what did we really learn from looking at workforce composition? If you think about it, this chapter was less about charts and more about uncovering the *hidden story* behind the people who keep an organization running. Here are the big lessons that stand out:

- **Diversity is a secret weapon** – When everyone comes from the same academic background, you end up with the same ideas. Mix in engineers, designers, finance minds, and even arts graduates, and suddenly, innovation has room to breathe.
- **Experience is like seasoning** – Too many freshers? You'll spend months training. Too many veterans? You risk being stuck in "we've always done it this way." The sweet spot is the right blend.
- **Leadership representation matters** – Every time a woman or underrepresented group steps into senior management, it's not just a promotion—it's a signal to the whole company that growth is possible for everyone.

- **Generational balance is the safety net** – If a whole department is nearing retirement, that's a ticking clock. A good age mix means knowledge transfer, mentorship, and continuity.
- **Role mix keeps things agile** – Imagine a football team made up of only strikers. Exciting for a bit, but no one's defending the goal. Balanced job roles keep departments versatile and resilient.
- **Early exits are red flags** – When new hires leave too soon, you're not just losing people—you're losing tomorrow's managers. Fixing onboarding and career paths is key.
- **Geography tells a growth story** – Headcount spikes in one region usually mean the business is betting big there. Spotting that early helps HR plan resources before problems show up.
- **Structure shows the hidden truths** – Org charts aren't boring—they reveal whether teams are overloaded, under-supported, or simply too complex.
- **Gender balance = culture check** – It's not only about fairness; balanced teams are proven to perform better, think differently, and stay engaged.

☞ The bottom line: Workforce composition answers the question, *"Do we have the right people, in the right place, with the right balance?"*

With this, we wrap up Chapter 1: Workforce Composition. We've taken a snapshot of today's workforce. Next, we'll shift gears to Chapter 2: Workforce Planning & Forecasting, where the spotlight moves from *"who we have now"* to *"who we'll need tomorrow."*

CHAPTER 2

WORKFORCE PLANNING & FORECASTING

Section 1: Introduction

In today's fast-changing business environment, workforce planning continues to evolve from being a few-times-a-year HR exercise to an ongoing, business-critical activity. It is no longer just about counting how many employees an organization has who can deliver, but it is more about asking whether we have the *right number of people, in the right roles, at the right time*. This simple but powerful question lies at the heart of workforce planning and forecasting.

Workforce planning acts as the bridge between strategy and execution. If the business is planning to expand into a new region, launch a product, or take on a large project, HR must translate that vision into hiring plans, role transitions, and retention strategies. Forecasting adds another dimension—it introduces time and anticipation. Instead of reacting to vacancies, retirements, or sudden attrition, forecasting helps organizations prepare in advance, ensuring smooth operations without last-minute talent shortages.

Consider how impactful this can be: a company entering a growth market can ramp up recruitment early enough to meet demand, a business unit with high turnover can proactively adjust hiring pipelines, and a department facing a retirement wave can anticipate knowledge transfer needs. On the other hand, failing to forecast often results in project delays, overstretched teams, or even missed opportunities due to a lack of talent readiness.

What makes workforce planning unique is its dual perspective: it balances immediate staffing needs with long-term organizational sustainability. It uses historical data to understand workforce changes over time and applies predictive techniques to prepare for what's ahead. Done well, it not only answers "What just happened?" but also provides clarity on "What's next?" and "What should we do about it?"

This chapter explores the questions, insights, and real-world challenges that make workforce planning and forecasting a vital compass for HR and business leaders.

Section 2: Data Sources

Before we can forecast the workforce, we need to know where the data comes from. Think of it like preparing a weather forecast—you can't predict tomorrow's rain unless you track yesterday's clouds, today's wind, and wider climate patterns. Workforce planning works the same way. The "climate data" for HR comes from five main sources:

1. Human Resource Information System (HRIS)

This is the system of record for your workforce. It tracks hires, exits, department changes, job titles, and employment status. It's the foundation for understanding net workforce change over time.

☞ **Example:** If you want to see how many employees left the sales team last year versus how many joined, HRIS is where you pull the base data from.

2. Applicant Tracking System (ATS)

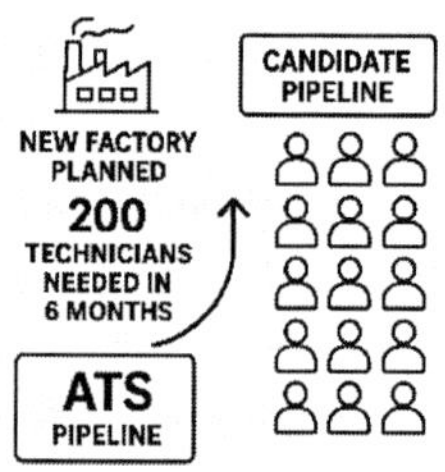

ATS data tells the story of hiring—volumes, timing, and sourcing of candidates. It helps connect recruitment activity with future workforce needs, especially when planning for expansions or project-based hiring.

☞ **Example:** If the company plans a new factory and needs 200 technicians in six months, ATS data shows whether the pipeline can deliver that volume in time.

3. Internal Mobility & Promotion Records

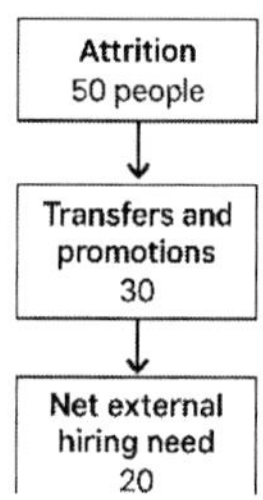

Not all workforce changes come from new hires. Internal moves, role changes, and promotions reshape departments constantly. This data shows whether the company is filling gaps with internal talent or relying heavily on external recruitment.

☞ **Example:** If attrition in IT is 50 people, but 30 were replaced through transfers and promotions, the net external hiring need is only 20.

4. Forecasting & Planning Tools

These tools project future headcount by factoring in retirements, attrition rates, and business growth plans. They're the "crystal ball" that turns raw numbers into forward-looking scenarios.

☞ **Example:** If 15% of engineers are due to retire in the next three years, these tools can flag the urgency for early recruitment.

5. Economic & Labor Market Data

Workforce trends don't exist in isolation. External data—like unemployment rates, GDP shifts, and industry hiring benchmarks—provides critical context for surges or freezes.

☞ **Example:** If GDP growth dips and industry-wide hiring slows, you may expect longer time-to-fill but lower attrition pressure.

When these sources are combined, HR leaders get both a rearview mirror (what's been happening) and a windshield (what's coming ahead). The real power lies not in looking at one dataset, but in connecting them to build a reliable workforce forecast.

Section 3: The Workforce Mirror – Stories & Strategic Questions

When FutureTech Inc. looked back at its workforce data, the story on the surface seemed impressive. In five years, the company doubled its headcount, spreading into new regions and launching fresh business units. The executive team proudly pointed to line charts showing consistent growth, using them as proof of success in every town hall. Yet, like many companies, FutureTech learned that headcount history can be deceiving. Growth in numbers alone did not mean stability, balance, or readiness for the future.

From 2018 to 2020, hiring surged aggressively, driven by an ambitious expansion strategy. But in 2021, growth slowed dramatically. Employees whispered that leadership had lost its vision. The truth was more nuanced—market conditions had changed, projects were delayed, and unplanned attrition had hit certain functions harder than expected. The graph of headcount over five years told the "what," but not the "why."

To understand the full picture of their growth, FutureTech needed to start with the foundational questions:

16. How has our total headcount changed in the past five years?
    – Reveals whether the organization is steadily growing, contracting, or fluctuating.
17. What are the most common reasons for year-over-year workforce growth or decline?
    – Shows whether hiring spikes, attrition, or restructuring are driving the changes.

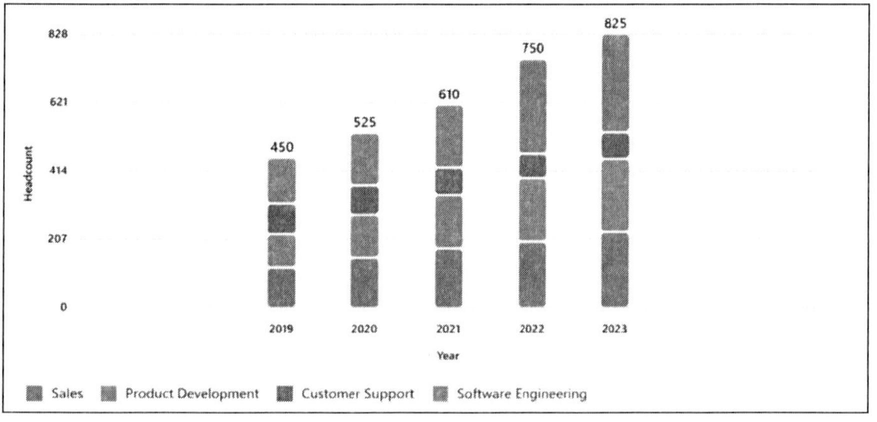

Graph 2.1: The Growth Story: Headcount Trends and Departmental Imbalances

The reasons behind year-over-year changes became the next big revelation. Some years, growth was fueled by large client wins that required mass hiring in tech and sales. In others, sudden exits from frustrated teams or global crises reduced staff numbers despite new hiring efforts. For example, when one year's attrition peaked in customer service, the department struggled to keep pace even though freshers were recruited in bulk.

Digging deeper, department-level data showed an uneven picture. Sales and product development experienced the fastest growth, while operations and support trailed behind. This imbalance created a lopsided organization: plenty of people to sell and build, but not enough to support clients once the deals were closed.

When the HR team analyzed annual net gain or loss by department, the picture grew clearer. A positive net gain in one unit often hid a quiet decline elsewhere. For instance, while the software engineering unit had a net gain of 150 employees in one year, customer support actually posted a net loss of 40. Clients only saw missed calls and delayed resolutions—they didn't care that "net company headcount" was positive.

To diagnose these dangerous imbalances, FutureTech turned to a more granular set of questions:

18. Which departments have experienced the most growth or decline?
    – Highlights where expansion is fueling capability—or where contraction may signal risk.
19. What is our annual net gain or loss of employees by department?
    – Balances hires, exits, and internal moves to see the true workforce shift.
20. Who contributes more to net change: new hires, internal transfers, or attrition?
    – Breaks down the mechanics of change so leaders know what's driving the numbers.

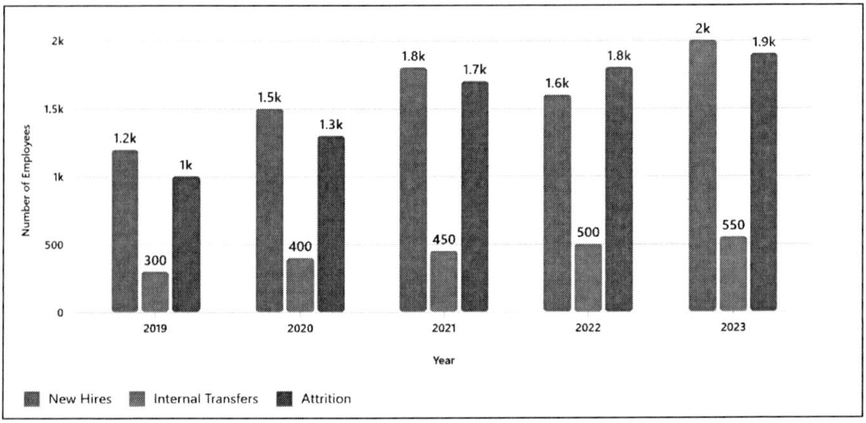

Graph 2.2: The Mechanics of Workforce Change: Growth, Decline, and the Retirement Risk

Another angle revealed who truly drove workforce change: new hires, internal transfers, or attrition. For years, leadership celebrated hiring figures as a sign of progress. But once HR broke it down, they saw that internal transfers contributed as much as 25% to workforce shifts, often leaving gaps behind in their previous teams. Worse, attrition sometimes outweighed new hiring, meaning that despite thousands of offers, the net workforce barely changed.

Then came the wake-up call of retirement forecasts. In manufacturing and R&D, some of the most experienced employees were about to retire within the next five years. A "knowledge drain" loomed, threatening not just numbers but decades of expertise. The company had no systematic plan to capture knowledge, and succession planning was patchy at best.

This forced FutureTech to confront the human element behind the numbers:

21. How do projected retirements influence our future staffing needs?

– Flags areas where experience gaps may emerge if knowledge isn't transferred in time.

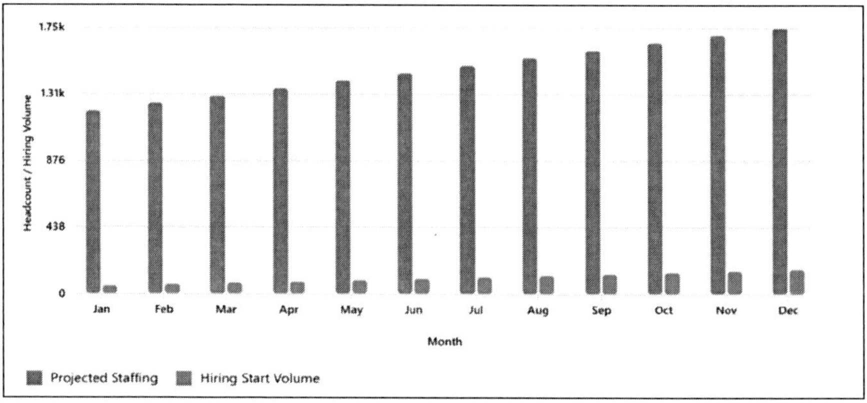

Graph 2.3: Forecasting the Human Factor: Staffing Needs and Timing Risks

Forecasting future size added another layer of complexity. Projections suggested steady growth over the next year, but when HR overlaid those forecasts with business milestones—like product launches and market expansions—they discovered gaps. Hiring timelines weren't aligned with strategic initiatives. In one painful example, a major product launch in Europe was delayed by six months simply because the sales and support teams weren't staffed on time.

The misalignment highlighted another issue—timing. Whenever skill shortages were anticipated, the company often started recruitment too late. For niche roles like cybersecurity specialists or data scientists, the lead time from sourcing to onboarding was months. Yet managers usually raised requisitions just weeks before projects began.

Even large-scale hiring pushes exposed timing challenges. When FutureTech won a government contract requiring 300 new hires in under six months, recruiters worked overtime. The rush led to shallow screenings, overwhelmed onboarding, and higher-than-usual attrition in the first three months.

To move from reactive to proactive, FutureTech had to master the art of forecasting and timing:

22. What is the projected size of our workforce next year?
    – Provides a forward-looking baseline for planning budgets, hiring, and skills.
23. How aligned are our hiring plans and business milestones?
    – Tests whether recruitment is paced correctly for major launches or growth phases.
24. How early do we need to start ramping up recruitment for anticipated skill shortages?
    – Helps prevent last-minute scrambles by mapping lead times.
25. How long does it take to ramp up for major hiring pushes?
    – Measures recruitment efficiency and capacity to handle scale.

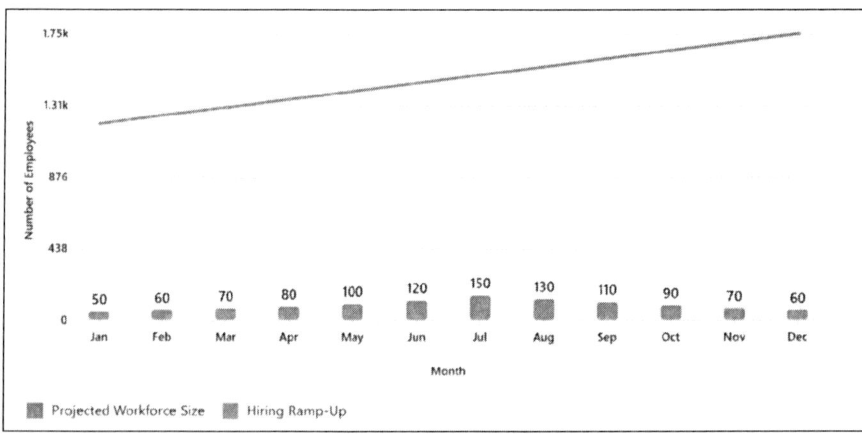

Graph 2.4: Forecasting Workforce Size and Timing Risks: Navigating Economic Cycles

External economic cycles also played a disruptive role. During the last recession, hiring froze overnight. HR leaders congratulated themselves on "managing costs," but attrition continued naturally. By the end of the freeze, teams were shrunken to critical lows. When the economy recovered, they tried to restart hiring, but it took months to rebuild momentum. Business opportunities slipped away because talent wasn't available fast enough.

The opposite happened during a boom. Flush with new projects, the company launched an aggressive hiring spree. Yet six months later, when client demand slowed, many of those hires were benched with no projects to work on. Costs ballooned, morale dropped, and layoffs followed.

Perhaps the most sobering analysis came when HR overlaid workforce trends with economic cycles from the past decade. The patterns were clear: during downturns, attrition slowed because employees stayed put, but hiring froze. During upturns, attrition spiked as competitors poached talent, while rushed hiring lowered quality. The workforce size graph moved almost in sync with the GDP chart.

To build true resilience, FutureTech learned to look beyond its own walls and ask:

26. Are our hiring surges or freezes correlated with economic indicators? – Links workforce changes to market realities like GDP shifts or downturns.
27. How did our hiring/attrition adjust during major economic cycles? – Provides lessons on resilience and adaptability for future planning.

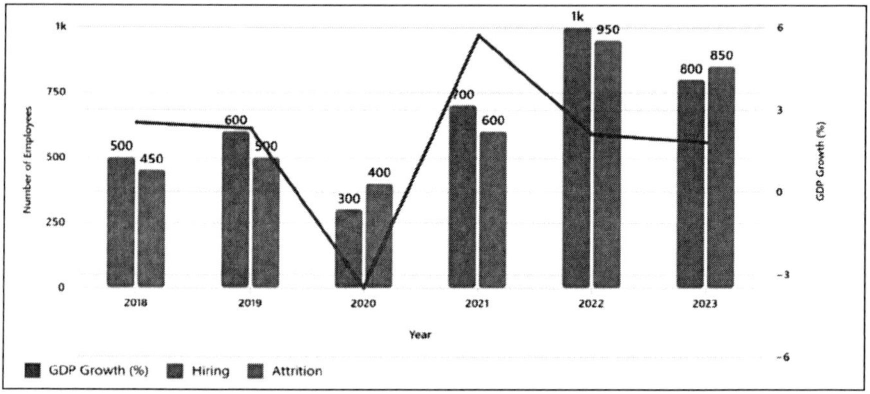

Graph 2.5: Economic Cycles and Workforce Resilience: Hiring and Attrition Trends at FutureTech

The Transformation: From Firefighting to Foresight

The lessons accumulated into one powerful realization. Workforce planning was not just about "how many people" a company had at any given time. It was about why headcount changed, where growth or decline was happening, who was driving the shifts, when recruitment should start, and how external forces influenced it all.

But the story didn't end with the problems. Slowly, FutureTech turned lessons into action. Annual planning began, including retirement forecasts, ensuring succession plans were in place before knowledge disappeared. Net gain analyses separated new hires, transfers, and attrition, giving leadership a clearer view of what was really changing the numbers. Hiring calendars were tied to business milestones, and economic scenario planning became part of workforce forecasting.

Over time, the company's narrative changed. Workforce data was no longer just about celebrating growth. By asking these 27 essential questions, FutureTech turned its workforce mirror into a window to the future—ready not just for today's demands but tomorrow's challenges.

Section 4: Key Takeaways

After exploring the stories behind workforce planning and forecasting, several key lessons emerge. These takeaways help HR leaders translate insights into action and ensure their organizations are prepared for both current operations and future challenges:

- **Understand Net Workforce Change**
  Break down annual headcount movement into hires, internal transfers, and attrition. This helps identify whether growth is sustainable or if internal shifts are masking functional gaps.
- **Link Workforce Trends to Business Milestones**
  Align hiring plans with product launches, expansion timelines, and strategic projects. Early recruitment planning prevents bottlenecks and ensures teams are ready when needed.
- **Plan for Retirements and Succession**
  Anticipate retirements to avoid sudden knowledge loss. Implement phased transitions, mentorship programs, and succession plans to maintain continuity.
- **Monitor Departmental Growth and Decline**
  Track which departments are expanding or contracting. Persistent imbalances indicate where resources, leadership, or support structures need attention.
- **Time Recruitment for Skill Shortages**
  Start ramping up hiring well before demand peaks. For niche roles, lead times are critical to avoid operational delays and compromised project delivery.
- **Track Ramp-Up Efficiency**
  Measure how quickly departments reach target headcount during large hiring pushes. Identify delays early and optimize onboarding and sourcing processes.

- **Correlate Workforce Changes with Economic Cycles**
  Understand how external factors—like recessions or booms—impact attrition, hiring surges, and freezes. Scenario planning reduces reactive decision-making.
- **Forecast vs. Reality**
  Compare projected workforce numbers against actuals. Large deviations highlight gaps in planning, data accuracy, or external shocks that require agile adjustments.
- **Balance Growth Across Functions and Locations**
  Ensure hiring is not concentrated in a single department or geography. Balanced distribution reduces operational risk and strengthens organizational resilience.
- **Treat Data as a Strategic Compass**
  Workforce metrics are more than numbers—they reveal timing, trends, and hidden risks. When interpreted proactively, they guide smarter decisions, better talent deployment, and long-term readiness.

Workforce planning is not about predicting the future perfectly — it's about being ready for it. From anticipating retirements to aligning hiring with business milestones, every decision adds to an organization's agility. When data reveals not just what changed but why it changed, HR moves from firefighting to foresight.

☞ The Bottom Line: Workforce planning answers the question:

"Are we growing in the right direction, at the right pace, with the readiness to meet what's coming next?"

With these insights as a foundation, we now turn to **Chapter 3: Skill Trends & Gaps**, where we explore how to identify, analyze, and act on the evolving skill needs of the workforce to stay competitive and future-ready.

CHAPTER 3

SKILL TRENDS & GAPS

Section 1: Introduction

In today's fast-paced business environment, having the right number of employees is no longer enough. The real advantage comes from having the right skills in the right place at the right time. While headcount metrics show how many people an organization employs, skill data reveals what they can actually do—and whether those capabilities align with current and future strategic needs. Ignoring this dimension can leave organizations staffed but unprepared, with talent gaps silently affecting productivity, innovation, and competitive advantage.

This chapter focuses on understanding skill trends and identifying gaps within the workforce. It addresses questions such as: Are we hiring talent that closes critical skill gaps? Which skills are in highest demand, and are internal training programs helping employees acquire them quickly? Are we building a workforce of specialists, generalists, or a balanced mix? By examining these areas, organizations can ensure that workforce development isn't reactive but anticipatory, equipping teams with the competencies necessary to achieve business goals.

Skill trend analysis also provides a forward-looking perspective. Rising demand for certain technical proficiencies, for example, may signal future recruitment needs, while tracking the speed of skill adoption highlights which training programs are most effective. Understanding these patterns enables HR leaders to make informed decisions on hiring, upskilling, and talent mobility, reducing reliance on costly external hires and accelerating organizational capability.

Ultimately, aligning skills with business priorities transforms workforce planning from a numbers exercise into a strategic capability. By systematically measuring skill trends, identifying gaps, and taking targeted action, organizations can ensure that the right people, with the right skills, are ready to meet both current operational demands and future growth opportunities.

Section 2: Data Sources

Before we can analyze skill trends and gaps, we need to know where the data comes from. Think of it like diagnosing the health of a team—you can't fix weaknesses unless you first examine strength, endurance, and agility across all players. In HR, skill "health checks" rely on several key sources:

Human Resource Information System (HRIS)

This is the master record for workforce data. It tracks employees' roles, departments, grades, and tenure. HRIS forms the baseline for mapping which skills exist where, and which roles may be under- or over-equipped.

☞ Example: If you want to see how many developers have advanced coding certifications versus basic skills, HRIS is where you start.

Skills Inventory & Competency Databases

These systems capture employee skill levels, certifications, and competencies. They reveal gaps between current capabilities and what roles actually require.

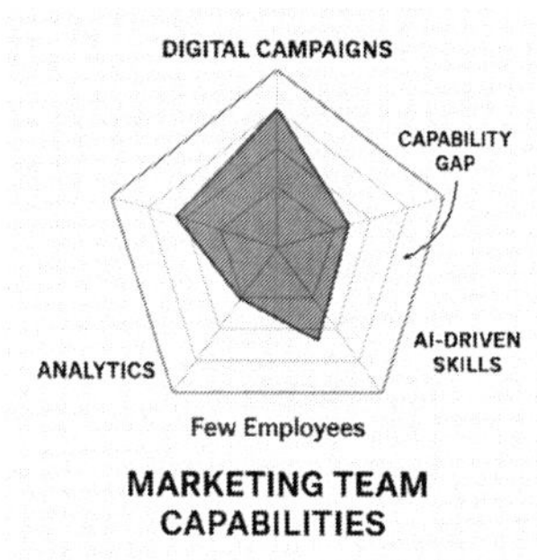

☞ Example: A radar chart might show that while marketing teams excel in digital campaigns, few employees have analytics or AI-driven skills—highlighting a capability gap.

Recruitment & Job Posting Data

Data from ATS or job boards indicates which skills are being sought in new hires. It connects hiring activity to organizational skill needs, showing whether recruitment is addressing critical gaps.

☞ Example: If most new job postings ask for cloud computing expertise, HR can check whether internal employees are being upskilled or if external hiring is required.

Learning & Development (L&D) Platforms

L&D platforms track course enrollments, completion, and skill assessments. They show

how quickly employees adopt new capabilities and which programs are most effective.

☞ Example: A line chart could track adoption speed for a cybersecurity course, indicating whether training reduces the need for external hires.

Manager Surveys & Skills Requests

Managers provide insight into unmet skill needs that might not appear in HRIS or training data. These subjective inputs highlight gaps critical to project delivery and growth.

☞ Example: Managers might request advanced analytics or design thinking skills that current teams lack, signaling a priority for hiring or training.

External Labor Market Data

Industry trends and competitor hiring patterns provide context for internal capability planning. They indicate emerging skills needed to remain competitive.

☞ Example: If AI-related skills are surging in the industry, the organization can proactively build capabilities before gaps impact projects.

By combining these sources, HR leaders get both a clear picture of current skill capabilities and an early warning system for emerging gaps. The power lies in connecting the data, not just collecting it—so workforce planning can be truly capability-driven.

Section 3: The Skill Gap Mirror – From Reactive Panic to Proactive Capability

The Illusion of Competence

BrightTech had long been a favorite of the tech sector, a company that prided itself on steady growth and a robust, ever-expanding headcount. Every quarter, a fresh cohort of bright-eyed graduates and seasoned professionals passed through its doors, while its internal university boasted an impressive catalog of training programs. On the surface, the workforce was a well-oiled machine, its strength reflected in rising employee numbers and healthy recruitment metrics. The leadership team, confident in their human capital, greenlit an ambitious new strategy: a suite of advanced, AI-driven products designed to catapult them into a new league of innovation.

The first cracks in this façade appeared not as a collapse, but as a persistent, nagging drag on velocity. Project leads in the AI division began reporting a curious pattern. They had plenty of data scientists—the headcount was perfect—yet their most promising models were stalling. Prototypes that shone in testing environments faltered when faced with the complexities of real-world deployment. The issue wasn't a lack of theoretical knowledge; it was a stark absence of practical, production-grade expertise. Teams understood algorithms but struggled with the intricate plumbing of **MLOps**—the continuous integration and deployment pipelines needed to keep AI models alive, learning, and accurate in a live environment. Furthermore, a critical gap in **cloud architecture** meant they couldn't efficiently scale their computations, and a lack of deep **algorithm optimization** skills made their models slow and costly to run.

This was BrightTech's moment of reckoning. They had been counting heads, not capabilities. The projects weren't failing due to a lack of people, but due to a fundamental misalignment between the skills they had and the skills they needed to execute their strategy. The company's future was being held hostage by invisible skill gaps.

The first, and most humbling, question they had to answer was:

28. What are the top three skill gaps in the current workforce?
    – This moves beyond vague concerns to a precise diagnosis, revealing the critical capabilities that are actively limiting project delivery, innovation, and strategic growth. For BrightTech, the answer was unequivocal: MLOps, cloud architecture, and algorithm optimization.

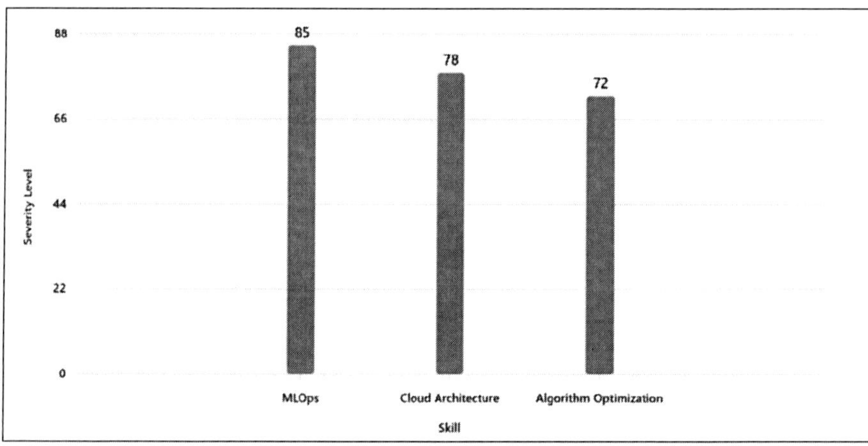

Graph 3.1: BrightTech's Skill Gaps: A Capability Crisis

The Hiring Mirage: Filling Seats, Not Gaps

In response to the crisis, HR was tasked with a hiring surge. Recruitment teams worked tirelessly, and the influx of new employees continued. For a moment, it seemed the problem was being solved. But a more nuanced analysis revealed a disturbing trend. The majority of new hires were bright generalists—excellent coders with strong foundational knowledge, but few possessed the specialized, niche expertise required to untangle the complex knots in the AI pipeline.

This exposed a critical flaw in their talent acquisition strategy. They were measuring success by offers accepted and time-to-fill, not by the strategic closure of capability deficits. They were filling seats, but the seats were not the right ones for the task at hand. The "skills" column on their HR spreadsheet was too generic, listing "Python" and "Machine Learning" instead of "Kubernetes for ML workload orchestration" or "model drift detection and management."

This forced the organization to ask a more penetrating question about their talent pipeline:

29. Are our new hires closing the most critical skill gaps?
    – This question shifts the focus of recruitment from volume to impact. It reveals whether the talent acquisition engine is strategically aligned with the company's most urgent capability shortages or merely adding to the numbers. For BrightTech, the answer was a resounding "no," prompting a complete overhaul of their job descriptions, sourcing strategies, and interview rubrics to target experienced specialists who could hit the ground running.

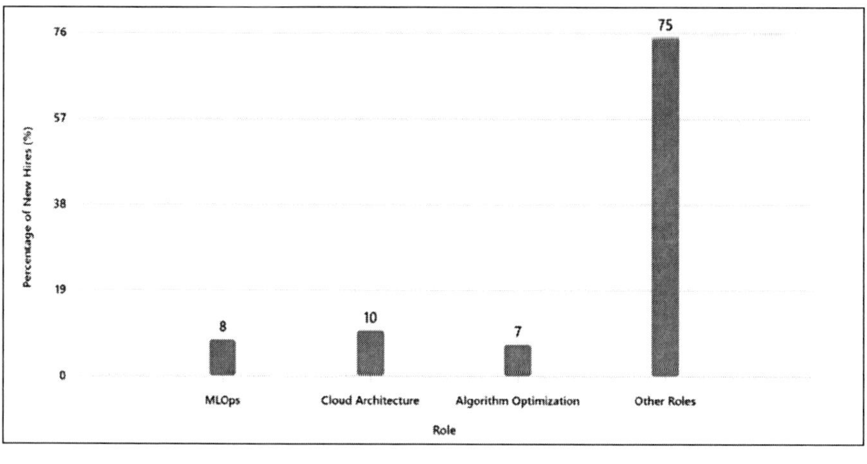

Graph 3.2: Are New Hires Closing the Skill Gaps? BrightTech's Recruitment Misalignment

Listening to the Whisper of Future Needs

As BrightTech began to course-correct its immediate hiring, a new pattern emerged from conversations with line managers. In project kick-off meetings and resource-planning sessions, team leads were consistently requesting skills that simply didn't exist within the company's walls. These weren't the gaps of today, but the essential capabilities for tomorrow. Managers were asking for expertise in **AI explainability** to meet upcoming regulatory requirements, **data ethics compliance** to build trust with customers, and mastery of nascent **reinforcement learning frameworks** for the next product generation.

These requests were like early-warning tremors before a major seismic shift. They signaled that even if BrightTech solved today's MLOps crisis, they would be just as vulnerable tomorrow without a new set of capabilities. The internal workforce, left to its own devices, could not organically grow these highly specialized skills fast enough.

To anticipate the next crisis, they began systematically tracking:

30. What new skills are being requested by managers that we cannot yet provide internally?
    – This question transforms informal manager frustrations into a strategic early-warning system. It highlights emerging skill needs that demand proactive investment, whether through targeted hiring, strategic partnerships, or bespoke reskilling programs, ensuring the organization isn't constantly playing catch-up.

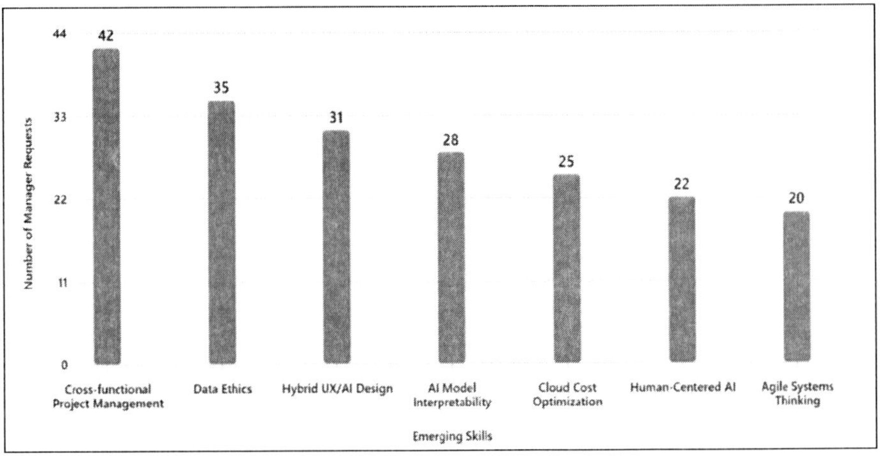

Graph 3.3: BrightTech's Emerging Skill Needs and the Specialist Trap

The Specialist Trap: Depth at the Cost of Agility

In their push to hire specialists to solve the immediate gaps, BrightTech inadvertently created a new problem: organizational silos. Their teams became populated with world-class experts who spoke in deep, but narrow, dialects. The MLOps engineer was brilliant at deployment but couldn't dialogue effectively with the data ethicist. The cloud architect optimized for cost and performance but was disconnected from the UX designer who understood how model latency impacted user retention.

This over-reliance on specialists created bottlenecks and friction. Projects progressed in fits and starts, handed off between teams like a relay race where the runners had never practiced passing the baton. The organization had immense depth but lacked the connective tissue—the generalists and hybrid professionals—who could translate between domains, manage cross-functional projects, and ensure that deep expertise was effectively integrated into a cohesive final product.

This forced a strategic conversation about the very DNA of their workforce:

31. Are we trending toward hiring more specialists or generalists?
   – This is not about choosing one over the other, but about intentional design. The answer informs organizational structure, succession planning, and innovation capacity. A specialist-heavy workforce offers deep expertise but can be inflexible; a generalist-heavy one is agile but may lack cutting-edge capability. BrightTech realized they needed a balanced portfolio, intentionally hiring "T-shaped" professionals with deep expertise in one area but broad collaborative skills across many.

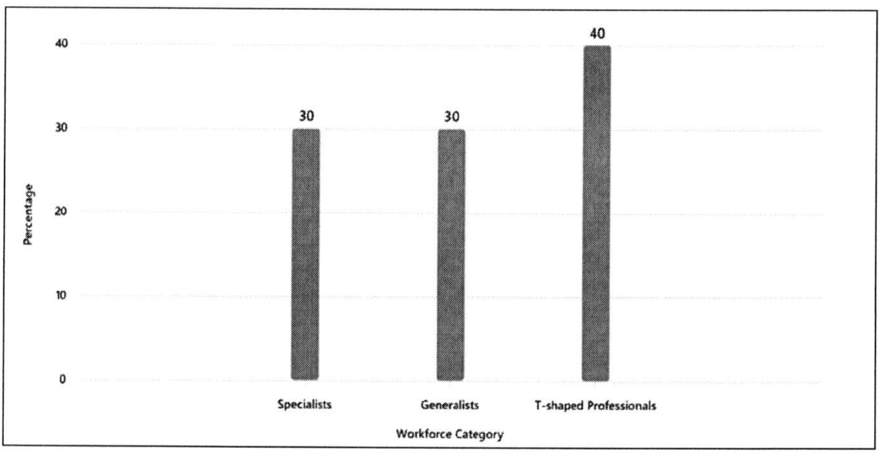

Graph 3.4: Strategic Workforce Design: Balancing Specialists and Generalists

Measuring the ROI of Learning

With millions invested in its internal "BrightTech University," the company had to ask: was it working? Some programs, like a hands-on "Cloud Fundamentals for Data Teams" workshop, showed spectacular results.

Participants immediately applied the learnings, shaving days off project deployment times. The skill adoption was rapid and measurable.

Other, more theoretical courses on topics like "Advanced AI Ethics" saw low enrollment and little observable impact on work. The problem wasn't the topic's importance, but the course's inability to translate theory into practice. By analyzing this disparity, BrightTech realized that training effectiveness wasn't a given; it had to be engineered and measured. They began to evaluate programs not by attendance or satisfaction scores, but by a "Skills Adoption Score"—a metric tracking the application of new learning on the job within 90 days.

This led to a more disciplined approach to development:

32. Which internal training programs see the fastest skill adoption?
    – This question identifies the high-impact programs that genuinely build capability and offer the highest return on investment. It allows L&D teams to double down on what works, redesign or retire what doesn't, and ensure that every dollar and hour spent on training translates into tangible performance improvement and reduced dependency on external hiring.

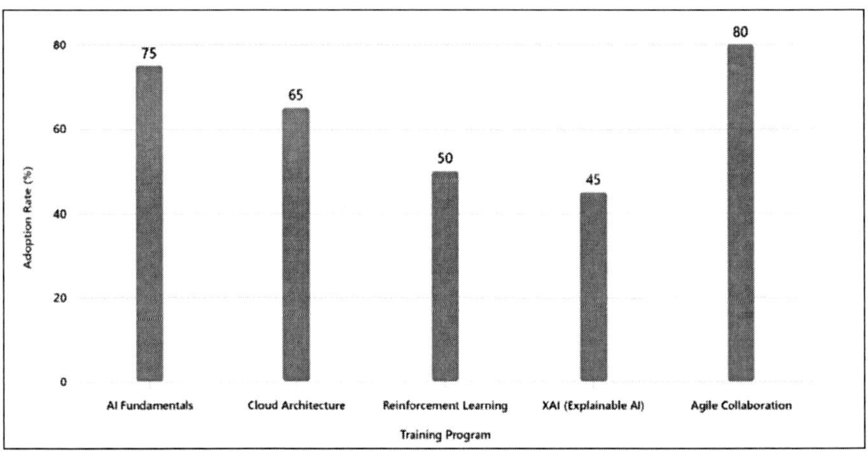

Graph 3.5: Fastest Skill Adoption in Internal Training Programs

The External Compass: Navigating the Market

Finally, BrightTech turned its gaze outward. An analysis of thousands of job postings from their main competitors revealed a clear picture of the evolving market. Skills like "AI Explainability (XAI)," "Reinforcement Learning," and "Cloud-Native Architecture" weren't just BrightTech's priorities; they were the industry's battleground. This external benchmarking was a reality check. It showed them which of their internal skill gaps were also industry-wide scarcities (and would therefore be more expensive and competitive to hire for) and revealed emerging trends they had not yet internally identified.

This allowed them to move from a reactive posture—"we need this skill because a project is stuck"—to a proactive one—"we need to build this skill because the market is demanding it, and we will need it for our 18-month strategy."

To complete their strategic view, they consistently asked:

33. Which skills are most frequently listed in recent job postings?
    – This provides an external compass. It offers invaluable insight into how the competition is building their teams and validates or challenges internal priorities. By aligning their internal skill development with external market trends, BrightTech ensured they remained competitive in the war for talent and were building a workforce ready for the future, not just the present.

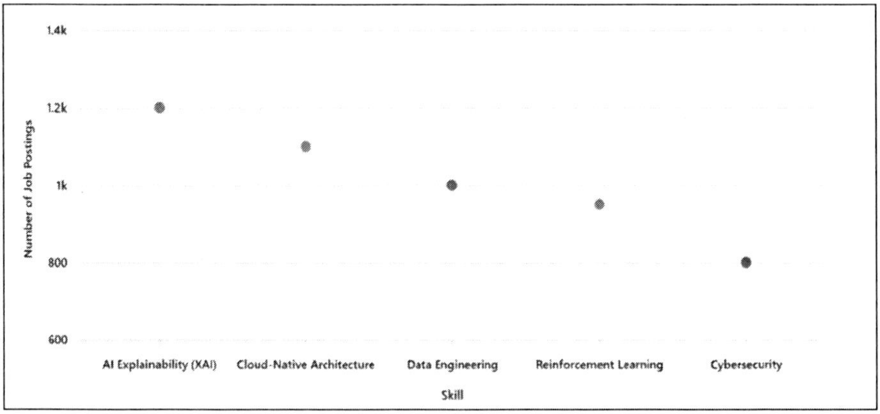

Graph 3.6: Skill Frequency in Job Postings

The Transformation: Building a Living, Breathing Capability System

BrightTech's journey from panic to prowess was not achieved by a single silver bullet. It was the result of treating skills not as a static checklist, but as a dynamic, living system that required constant monitoring and investment. By the end of their transformational year, they had not only closed the critical MLOps gap but had also built a resilient framework for continuous capability development.

Employees reported higher engagement, seeing a clear commitment to their growth and a direct line between their development and the company's most exciting work. Project delays decreased dramatically, and the company regained its confidence to tackle ambitious roadmaps.

The narrative of BrightTech underscores a fundamental truth: in the modern economy, workforce readiness is not a function of headcount. It is a function of the precise alignment between employee capabilities and strategic goals. By embedding these six essential questions into its regular HR and business planning rhythms, BrightTech transformed its approach. They moved from passively observing skill gaps to proactively building the capabilities that would define their future, ensuring that their human capital was not just a cost on a balance sheet, but their most potent and adaptable competitive advantage.

Section 4: Key Takeaways

So, what did we really learn from looking at skill trends and gaps? If you think about it, this chapter was less about counting heads and more about understanding what those people can actually do—and whether those capabilities are enough to meet today's and tomorrow's business needs. Here are the big lessons that stand out:

- **Critical skills drive performance** – Having a full team is good, but having the right skills is even better. Identify the top skill gaps first, because leaving them unaddressed can stall projects and slow growth.
- **Hiring must align with capability needs** – Bringing in new employees without the skills that matter most creates a mismatch. Targeted hiring ensures that gaps are closed faster and knowledge spreads across the team.
- **Emerging skills are early warning signals** – When managers request skills your workforce doesn't yet have, it's a heads-up for the future. Acting early with training or specialized hires keeps the company ahead of demand.
- **Balance specialists and generalists** – Specialists bring depth; generalists bring flexibility. A team full of either can create bottlenecks. The sweet spot is a mix that supports both expertise and cross-functional collaboration.
- **Training matters, but measure it** – Not all programs are equally effective. Focus on courses with high adoption rates and redesign those that lag, so learning truly translates into capability.

- **Market trends inform strategy** – Analyzing external demand for skills through job postings helps anticipate shortages. This way, hiring and upskilling are proactive, not reactive.
- **Skills are the real currency** – Beyond headcount, it's workforce capability that determines readiness. Teams that actively close skill gaps are faster, more agile, and better equipped for innovation.

☞ **The bottom line:** Skill trends and gaps answer the question, "Do we have the right people, with the right skills, in the right place?"

With this, we wrap up Chapter 3: Skill Trends & Gaps. We've examined not just what employees exist, but what they can do. Next, we'll shift gears to **Chapter 4: Internal Movement, Promotions & Career Paths**, where the focus moves from skills to growth—how employees move, progress, and build careers inside the organization.

CHAPTER 4

INTERNAL MOVEMENT, PROMOTIONS & CAREER PATHS

Section 1: Introduction

In any organization, growth isn't just about hiring new talent—it's also about how existing employees move, progress, and develop within the company. Internal movements, promotions, and well-defined career paths are the gears that keep the workforce engine running smoothly. Without clear insights into these dynamics, organizations risk misaligned aspirations, bottlenecked promotions, and unexpected talent gaps.

This chapter explores the intricate patterns of internal mobility and career progression. By asking questions such as, "How do employee aspirations align with business growth paths?" or "Which roles will see the most future hiring demand?", HR leaders can connect individual goals with organizational strategy. This ensures that high performers are retained, leadership pipelines remain strong, and departments are staffed for both current operations and future expansion.

Tracking promotion speed, internal transfers, and role transition patterns provides another layer of insight. Rapid promotions may signal exceptional talent but can create temporary shortages in key roles, while frequent

internal transfers may strengthen employee engagement but disrupt departmental headcount stability. Understanding which job levels see the fastest promotions and which functions experience the highest movement allows organizations to plan succession, training, and hiring strategies proactively.

Succession planning and leadership readiness are also central to workforce stability. Identifying feeder roles for senior positions, tracking participation in leadership development programs, and quantifying employees nearing retirement age helps mitigate the risk of sudden talent gaps. By combining these insights with visual tools—such as alluvial diagrams, Sankey flows, and hierarchical charts—organizations can see both the current talent flow and forecast where interventions are needed.

Ultimately, understanding internal movement and career pathways ensures that employees can grow while the organization continues to thrive. The goal is simple: align aspirations with opportunities, promote from within strategically, and maintain a pipeline of capable leaders to secure both present performance and future readiness.

Section 2: Data Sources

Before analyzing internal movement, promotions, and career paths, it's essential to understand where the data comes from. Think of it as mapping the currents in a river—you need to know how water flows to predict where it will go. Similarly, workforce progression and internal mobility can only be measured accurately with multiple integrated data sources.

Human Resource Information System (HRIS)

HRIS provides the baseline for internal movements, promotions, tenure, and reporting lines. It captures employees' current roles, job levels, and departmental assignments—crucial for understanding promotion pipelines and internal mobility trends.

Marketing Promotions Last Year

HRIS shows the history of job changes and timrelines.

Name	Previous Position	New Position	Date Promoted
Annette Black	Marketing Coordinator	Marketing Specialist	April 10, 2023
Jerome Bell	SEO Specialist	SEO Manager	Jul 18, 2023
Cameron Williamson	Content eator	Content Manager	Aug. 5, 2023
Kristin Watson	Senior Marketing Analyst	Marketing Manager	Oct. 30, 2023

☞ Example: To see which employees were promoted last year within the marketing team, HRIS shows the history of job changes and timelines.

Performance & Talent Management Systems

These track appraisals, performance scores, and succession readiness. They help identify high-potential employees, map feeder roles for leadership, and measure promotion eligibility.

☞ Example: If a department has multiple high performers but limited internal promotion, this may highlight a potential bottleneck.

Internal Mobility Records

Data on transfers, cross-functional moves, and secondments reveals how talent flows between teams. Monitoring these movements helps assess whether employees thrive post-transfer and how such shifts impact retention and departmental stability.

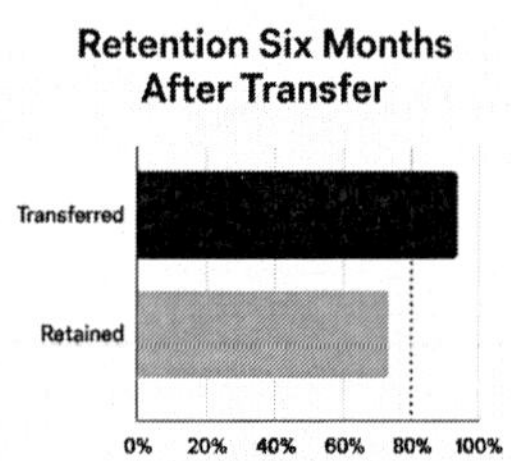

☞ Example: Tracking retention six months after a transfer shows whether internal moves are effective in retaining talent.

Learning & Development Platforms

L&D platforms track participation in training programs, leadership development, and succession initiatives. These insights show which employees are ready for advancement and how training impacts promotion rates.

☞ Example: Comparing promotion rates of employees who completed succession programs versus those who haven't highlights the program's effectiveness.

Organizational Charts & Hierarchy Data

Org charts reveal layers between frontline staff and executives, managerial bottlenecks, and career path breadth. They help visualize structural constraints that affect promotions and internal mobility.

☞ Example: If too many layers separate junior employees from senior roles, it may slow career progression and impact engagement.

By integrating these sources, HR can see both the **current state of internal movement** and **future opportunities for career progression**, enabling data-driven decisions that strengthen retention, fill key roles internally, and align employee aspirations with organizational needs.

Section 3: The Internal Mobility Mirror – From Chaotic Moves to Strategic Career Pathways

TechNova, a mid-sized software and cloud solutions company, had grown rapidly over the last five years. Its headcount charts pointed skyward, yet a quiet unease permeated the organization. Projects were delayed, key teams were stretched thin, and unexpected talent gaps in leadership were beginning to hamper strategic initiatives. It became clear that growth in numbers was not the same as growth in capability. The real story, they discovered, was hidden in the patterns of internal movement, promotions, and career pathways.

The investigation began with a simple survey, but the findings were profound. They discovered that while a majority of employees aspired to move into traditional people-leadership roles, TechNova's strategic plan called for an influx of experts in highly technical domains like cloud architecture leads, data platform managers, and AI specialists. There was a fundamental disconnect; the career paths employees dreamed of were not the ones the business critically needed to survive.

This misalignment prompted TechNova to ask a foundational strategic question:

34. How do employee aspirations align with business growth paths?
    – This highlights whether employees see opportunities in the roles the organization needs to fill. Misalignment, as TechNova found, is a direct path to future talent gaps and widespread disengagement.

To address this, HR began mapping career interests to strategic needs, providing employees with clear visibility into how their goals could intersect with organizational demand. This was no longer just about promotion; it was about purposeful movement.

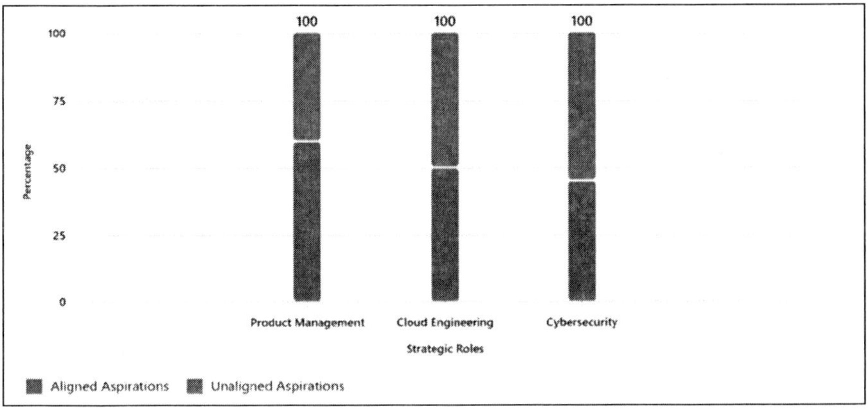

Graph 4.1: Alignment of Employee Aspirations with Strategic Growth Roles

With the aspiration gap identified, TechNova turned its gaze forward. Workforce forecasts painted a clear picture: the highest hiring demand over the next three years would be in product management, cloud engineering, and cybersecurity. This wasn't just a recruiting problem; it was a development imperative. If these roles were the future, they needed to become the focus of internal career pathing.

This analysis forced a critical, forward-looking question:

35. Which roles will see the most future hiring demand?
    – Identifying these positions early allows an organization to pivot its internal development, mentoring, and succession planning efforts to build from within, reducing dependency on expensive and risky external hires.

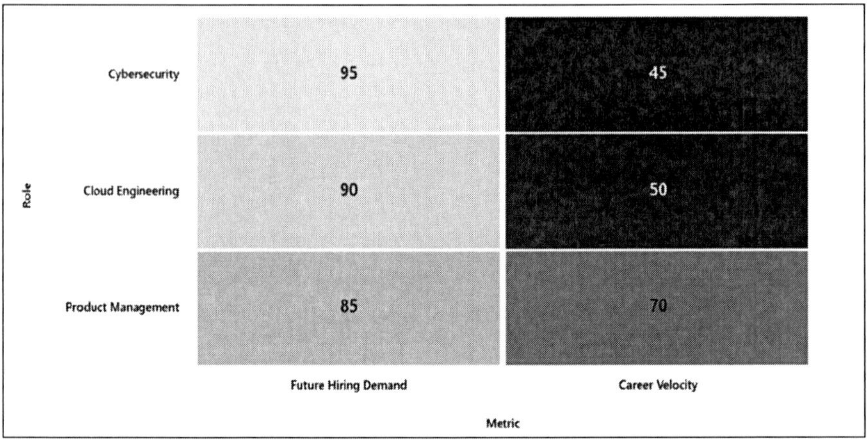

Graph 4.2: Future Hiring Demand vs Career Velocity

As they dug into the data, distinct patterns in career velocity emerged. Promotions were happening fastest in the sales and customer success departments, where high turnover and rapid growth created a conveyor belt of advancement. In contrast, the technology and engineering tracks followed a slower, more deliberate progression. This created a lopsided organization where some departments were constantly backfilling junior roles while others amassed experienced talent with limited upward mobility.

To understand the mechanics of this movement, TechNova analyzed two key dimensions:

36. In which departments do employees get promoted fastest?
    – This reveals where rapid advancement may be creating experience gaps or overpressuring newly promoted middle managers.
37. Which job levels have the shortest average time to promotion?
    – This indicates levels with accelerated movement, serving as an early warning system to plan for imminent vacancies and ensure proper training for those moving up.

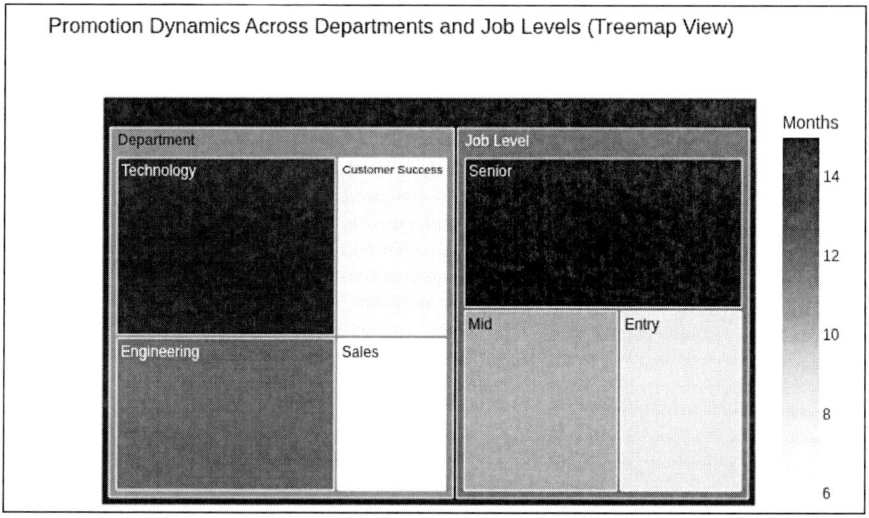

Graph 4.3: Promotion Dynamics Across Departments and Job Levels

The story grew more complex when TechNova examined lateral movement. They discovered that functions like IT support and business operations were hubs of internal transfers. More importantly, employees who moved into new departments showed significantly higher retention rates than their static peers. Internal mobility was not just a logistical event; it was a powerful antidote to attrition, fostering engagement and building a more versatile, resilient workforce.

This revelation shifted the focus from just upward mobility to holistic movement:

38. Are internal transfers resulting in higher retention in new departments?
    – This measures whether moving employees internally is a genuine retention tool, supporting engagement and long-term workforce stability.
39. Which functions have the highest rates of internal transfers?

– This pinpoints movement hotspots, which are crucial for accurate headcount planning and for understanding which departments act as talent incubators for the wider organization.

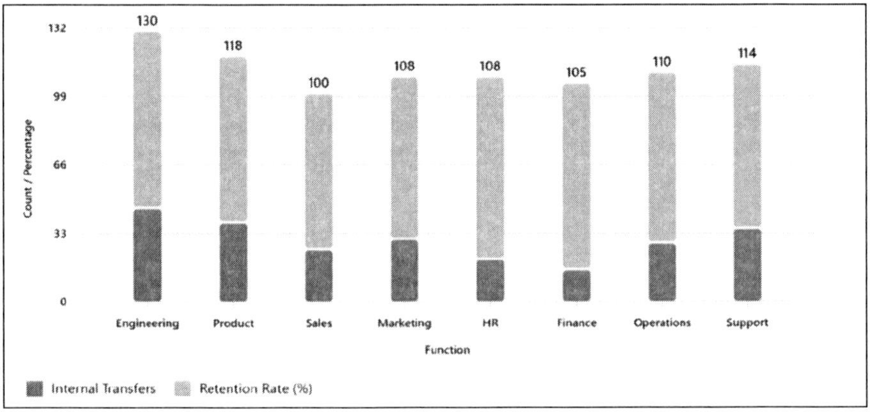

Graph 4.4: Internal Transfers and Retention Rates Across Functions at TechNova

Beneath all this movement lay the structural skeleton of the company itself. TechNova found that, on average, six layers of hierarchy separated a frontline employee from an executive. In the product development org, this structure was creating tangible bottlenecks: a handful of senior managers were overseeing sprawling teams, which slowed decision-making to a crawl and created a traffic jam for high-potential employees waiting for their chance to lead.

This led to a deep dive into organizational design:

40. How many organizational layers separate frontline employees from executives?
    – This assesses hierarchy depth and identifies potential structural barriers to communication and career progression.
41. Where are the biggest managerial bottlenecks in our org structure?

– This identifies overloaded managers or teams that are actively slowing down decision-making and stifling the growth of their reports.

42. Which business units offer the broadest choices for upward movement?

    – This shows which areas provide more robust career pathways, directly improving retention and satisfaction, and serving as a model for other parts of the business.

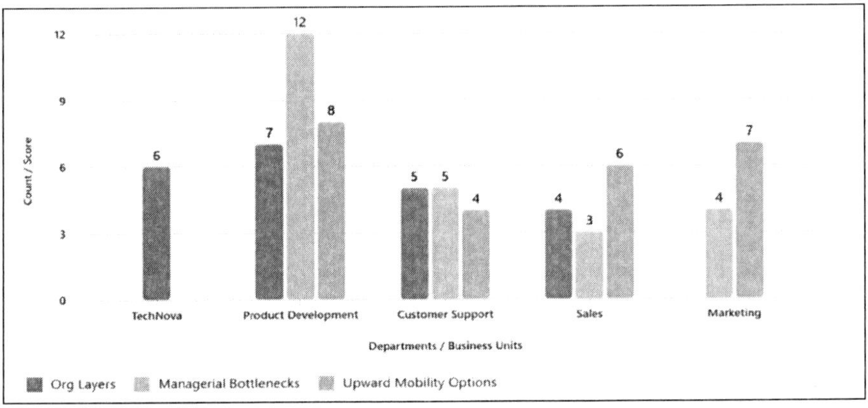

Graph 4.5: Designing for Growth: Structural Insights into TechNova's Organizational Mobility and Leadership Pipeline

Perhaps the most validating finding for TechNova's culture was the performance data. When they compared internally promoted employees to external hires in similar roles, the homegrown talent often performed at equal or higher levels. Furthermore, they found that 60% of their leadership roles were filled from within, a testament to a strong cultural pipeline.

To validate and refine their talent strategy, they asked:

43. Is performance higher among promoted or externally hired candidates?

– This comparison is vital for guiding hiring and promotion strategy, revealing the relative effectiveness and cultural integration of internal versus external talent.

44. What share of leadership roles are filled through internal promotions? – This indicates the organization's reliance on and health of its internal talent pipeline, a key metric for cultural continuity and succession health.

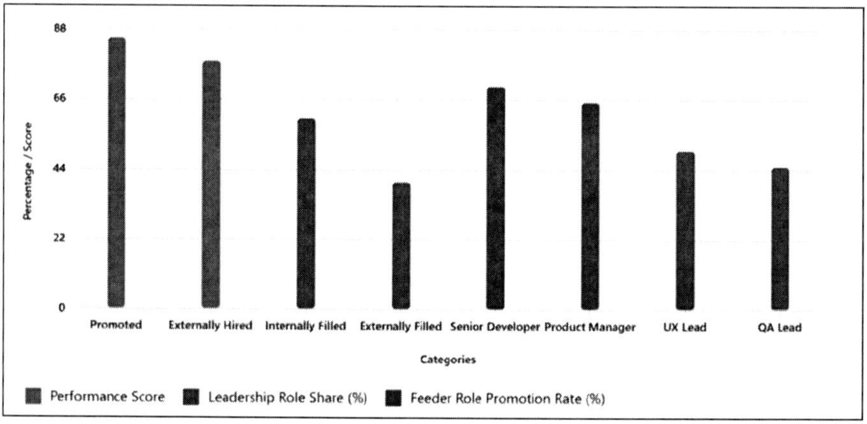

Graph 4.6: Building from Within: Performance, Leadership, and Promotion Pathways

The final piece of the puzzle was building a predictive model for succession. TechNova analyzed tenure data and found that employees typically remained in a role for 18-24 months before moving. They identified key "feeder roles"—like Senior Developer and Product Manager—that were the most common launching pads for leadership positions. They also confirmed that participation in formal succession planning strongly correlated with higher promotion rates. However, a looming threat was identified: 15% of their workforce, heavily concentrated in senior management, was nearing retirement.

To future-proof the organization, TechNova implemented a rigorous succession planning discipline built on these questions:

45. How long do employees typically remain in each job level before moving?
    – This provides insights into role tenure, enabling proactive succession planning and reducing the risk of unexpected vacancies.
46. What are the most common 'feeder' roles for senior leadership positions?
    – This maps the critical career pipelines for succession planning, allowing for targeted investment in development.
47. Does participation in succession planning correlate with higher promotion rates?
    – This evaluates the real-world effectiveness of leadership development programs.
48. How many employees are within five years of the expected retirement age?
    – This flags upcoming retirements, triggering proactive knowledge transfer and talent replacement strategies.
49. What is the completion rate of leadership training among succession candidates?
    – This tracks the readiness of future leaders and is a leading indicator of succession pipeline health.
50. Which departments have succession gaps for key roles?
    – This pinpoints urgent, high-risk areas where organizational continuity is threatened, demanding immediate intervention.

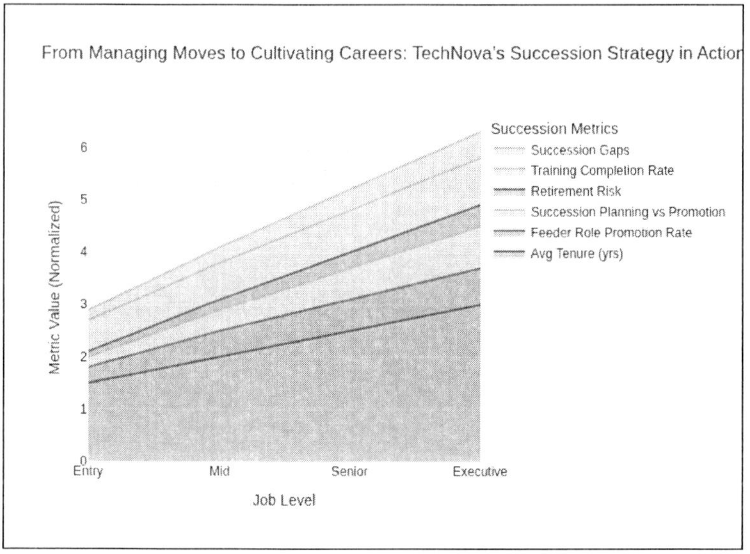

Graph 4.7: From Managing Moves to Cultivating Careers: TechNova's Succession Strategy in Action

The Transformation: From Managing Moves to Cultivating Careers

By the end of the year, TechNova had transformed its approach to internal mobility. It was no longer a series of administrative transactions but a strategic system for cultivating capability and commitment. Employees had clear visibility into growth opportunities that aligned with business needs, and managers had the data to backfill roles proactively and develop their people strategically.

The company's journey underscores a critical lesson: understanding internal movement is not about filling vacancies. It is about aligning the aspirations of your people with the needs of the business, ensuring continuity through robust succession planning, and using lateral and upward mobility as the primary engines of retention and engagement. By asking these seventeen essential questions, TechNova turned its internal mobility data into a strategic compass, guiding the organization toward a future where it was not just larger, but smarter, more agile, and deeply resilient.

Section 4: Key Takeaways

So, what did we really learn from exploring internal movement, promotions, and career paths at TechNova? If you think about it, this chapter wasn't just about who moved where—it was about uncovering how employees' growth journeys intersect with the organization's strategic needs. Here are the big lessons that stand out:

- **Career alignment drives continuity** – When employees' aspirations are mapped to roles in high-demand areas, both the individual and the organization win. Misalignment can create future talent gaps, while alignment ensures that succession pipelines remain healthy and critical roles are filled on time.
- **Forecasting future demand matters** – Knowing which roles will see the most hiring demand allows HR to prioritize training, internal mobility, and targeted recruitment. Planning prevents last-minute scrambles and ensures that projects stay on track.
- **Promotion velocity can reveal hidden gaps** – Rapid promotions in certain departments or job levels can leave intermediate layers understaffed. Tracking time-to-promotion by role and department helps identify where backfilling or succession planning is needed.
- **Internal mobility enhances retention** – Employees who transfer to new roles internally tend to stay longer and perform better. Encouraging lateral moves and cross-functional experience not only develops versatile talent but also stabilizes departmental headcount.
- **Hierarchy impacts agility** – Excessive layers between frontline employees and executives can slow decision-making and limit upward mobility. Identifying managerial bottlenecks helps redistribute

reporting responsibilities, ensuring smoother career progression and operational efficiency.

- **Breadth of career paths boosts engagement** – Units offering multiple upward and lateral movement options create more satisfied and motivated employees. Visibility into diverse career pathways reduces attrition and strengthens internal talent pipelines.
- **Promotions vs. external hires** – Internal promotions often match or exceed the performance of external hires. Relying on internal talent for leadership roles reinforces organizational knowledge, culture, and cost-efficiency.
- **Succession planning is essential** – Participation in leadership tracks correlates with higher promotion rates. Identifying potential retirements and succession gaps early ensures that critical roles are never left vacant and that the organization maintains continuity.
- **Feeder roles are the backbone** – Recognizing which positions consistently feed into leadership pipelines allows HR to focus mentoring and development efforts where they matter most.
- **Data-driven training strengthens readiness** – Tracking leadership program completion and succession metrics highlights gaps and guides targeted interventions, ensuring the workforce is prepared for future responsibilities.

☞ **The bottom line:** Internal movement, promotions, and career paths answer the question, "Are our people growing in ways that align with business needs, and is the organization prepared for the future?"

With this, we wrap up Chapter 4: Internal Movement, Promotions & Career Paths. We've mapped how employees move, grow, and prepare for the future. Next, we'll shift gears to Chapter 5: **Job Structure, Shifts & Scheduling**, where the spotlight moves from growth and career paths to **how roles are structured, schedules are managed, and shifts are organized** to optimize productivity, flexibility, and employee satisfaction.

CHAPTER 5

JOB STRUCTURE, SHIFTS & SCHEDULING

Section 1: Introduction

In today's fast-paced workplaces, productivity isn't just about having enough people—it's also about how roles are structured, shifts are scheduled, and workloads are distributed. Even the most capable workforce can struggle if schedules are misaligned, shifts are inflexible, or workload pressures are uneven. Understanding **job structure, shifts, and scheduling** is therefore critical to maintaining operational efficiency, employee well-being, and overall headcount effectiveness.

This chapter focuses on three interconnected dimensions: absenteeism and workload management, team interconnectivity, and the impact of shift patterns on retention and attrition. By asking questions such as, *"Does higher workload correspond to higher absenteeism?"* or *"Do flexible work schedules improve retention in shift-based roles?"*, organizations can uncover hidden operational risks and identify opportunities to optimize productivity.

Analyzing absenteeism alongside workload highlights units where employees may be overstretched. Chronic absenteeism not only reduces available headcount but can also signal underlying stress, burnout, or misalignment of responsibilities. Similarly, understanding which teams collaborate most across business verticals can reveal how interconnectivity either offsets or amplifies staffing challenges. Teams that work in isolation may experience bottlenecks, whereas cross-functional collaboration can help spread workload and increase efficiency.

Shift patterns are another critical factor in workforce stability. Organizations often rely on 24/7 operations, night shifts, or flexible schedules to maintain coverage. However, turnover rates can differ significantly between shifts, impacting headcount planning and recruitment needs. Flexible scheduling, on the other hand, may improve retention, particularly in shift-intensive roles, by supporting work-life balance and employee satisfaction.

By systematically measuring and visualizing these aspects—through scatter plots for absenteeism, heatmaps for team performance, and retention charts by shift type—HR leaders gain a comprehensive view of how job structures and scheduling practices affect both employee experience and operational readiness.

The goal is clear: ensure that roles are organized, shifts are managed, and workloads are balanced in a way that maintains **productivity, engagement, and workforce resilience**.

Section 2: Data Sources

Before we can optimize job structures, shifts, and schedules, we need to understand where the relevant data comes from. Think of it like managing a train network: to ensure all trains run on time, you need signals, schedules, and maintenance logs. In workforce management, HR relies on multiple data sources to see how roles, shifts, and workloads affect productivity and retention.

Human Resource Information System (HRIS)

HRIS provides the baseline for who is in each role, their reporting structure, and department assignments. It captures attendance records, shift allocations, and job classifications, helping to correlate workloads and absenteeism.

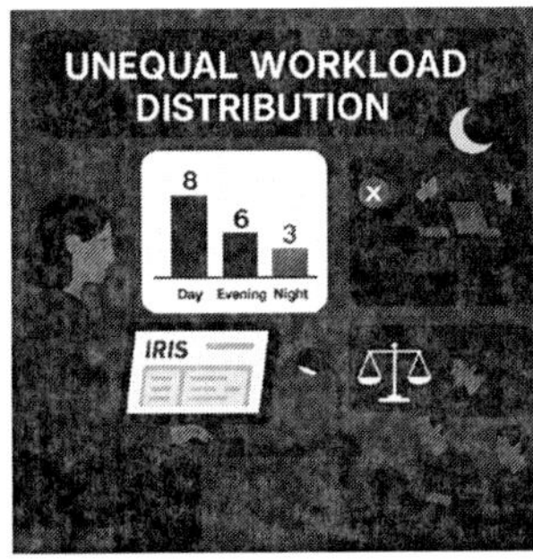

☞ Example: If a night shift team consistently shows high absenteeism, HRIS data allows tracking how many employees are assigned per shift and whether workload distribution is uneven.

Time & Attendance Systems

These platforms track clock-ins, clock-outs, and overtime hours. They help quantify workload pressures, identify absenteeism trends, and evaluate compliance with labor regulations.

☞ Example: By analyzing weekly overtime, HR can spot teams at risk of burnout or overload.

Workforce Scheduling Tools

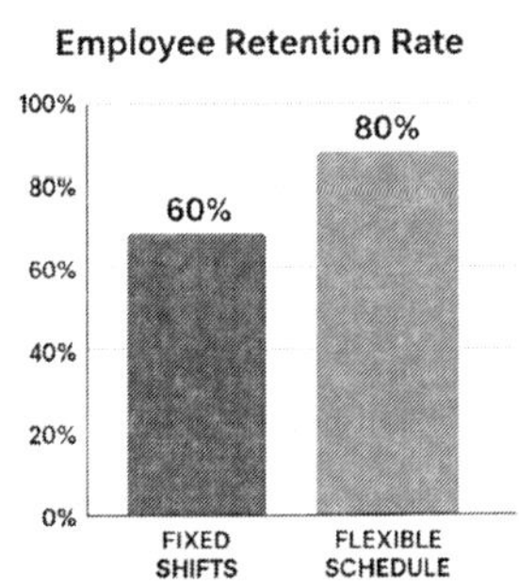

Scheduling systems record shift patterns, rotation schedules, and flexible work arrangements. They are critical to understanding how shift type or flexibility impacts retention and attrition.

☞ Example: Comparing retention rates of employees on fixed shifts versus flexible schedules highlights the effect of scheduling on employee satisfaction.

Collaboration & Team Interaction Data

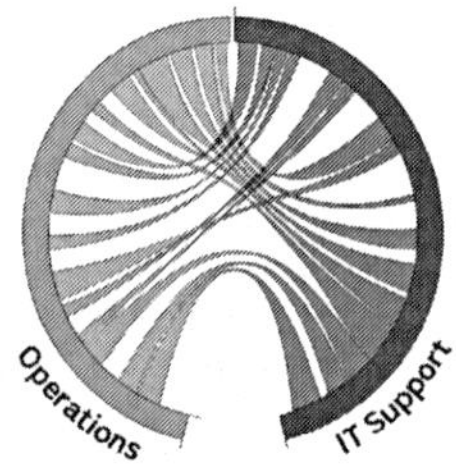

Captured through project management tools or internal communication platforms, this data maps cross-functional collaboration. It shows which teams are over-reliant on others or which functions act as isolated bottlenecks.

☞ Example: A chord diagram of interactions reveals if the operations team frequently depends on IT support, signaling potential overwork and workload dependency.

Employee Surveys & Feedback

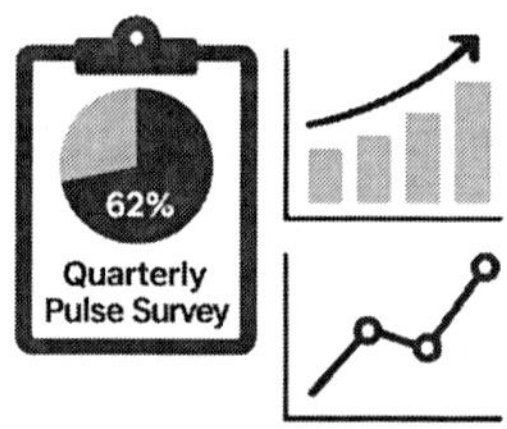

Pulse surveys or exit interviews provide qualitative insights into workload perception, shift satisfaction, and team collaboration. They complement quantitative data to explain why absenteeism or turnover occurs.

☞ **Example:** A quarterly pulse survey shows that 62% of employees in the customer support team report "frequent burnout due to unpredictable shifts." This aligns with rising absenteeism data from the same department, revealing that scheduling issues—not disengagement—are driving the problem.

When combined, these sources give HR a complete picture: not just who is working, but how, when, and under what conditions. The real value comes from connecting shift schedules, job structures, and workload patterns to operational outcomes—enabling smarter staffing, healthier teams, and more productive scheduling decisions.

Section 3: The Operational Pulse – Orchestrating Shifts, Well-being, and Resilience

In the high-stakes world of logistics, a fully staffed roster does not guarantee a smoothly running operation. This was the hard lesson learned by ShiftWorks, a mid-sized supply chain company whose distribution centers formed the backbone of its 24/7 business. On paper, their headcount was always met. In reality, the cracks were showing: delivery timelines stretched, overtime budgets ballooned, and a slow but steady drip of turnover was draining the company of experienced hands. The problem wasn't the number of people; it was the complex, often invisible, interplay between job structure, shift patterns, and human endurance. To survive, ShiftWorks had to learn to read the operational pulse of its workforce.

The Vicious Cycle: Workload and the Unplanned Absence

The investigation began with a hunch. Operations managers reported that during the peak holiday season, the same warehouse teams that processed record-breaking volumes also seemed to have the most people calling in sick. Was it a coincidence, or a pattern? To find out, HR plotted workload data—measured in parcels handled per hour—against absenteeism rates for every team over 12 months.

The resulting scatter plot was a revelation. It revealed a clear, upward-trending line, a direct correlation between sustained high workload and a spike in unplanned absences. The night shift at the Central Distribution Hub was the most glaring outlier. For weeks on end, the team operated at 130% of standard capacity, and their absenteeism rate soon doubled. This wasn't malingering; it was burnout manifesting as physical and mental exhaustion. Employees were literally making themselves sick to keep up, and then needing time to recover, which placed even more strain on those who remained.

This critical finding was rooted in a fundamental operational question:

51. Does higher workload correspond to higher absenteeism in any business units?
    – This reveals whether overworked teams are at risk of chronic absenteeism, which silently reduces effective headcount, erodes morale, and cripples productivity. For ShiftWorks, the answer was a definitive yes, transforming their view of absenteeism from an HR compliance issue to a real-time barometer of operational stress.

Diagnosing the Pain Points: From Data to Targeted Action

Armed with the knowledge that workload was a key driver, ShiftWorks needed to pinpoint the most vulnerable teams. They moved from a scatter plot to a heat map, visually layering average absenteeism rates over the organizational chart. The map lit up in red in three key areas: the night packing team, the pre-dawn driver dispatch team, and the returns processing department.

Seeing the problem concentrated so vividly allowed for targeted intervention. The night packing team, for instance, was subjected to a grueling schedule with minimal breaks. The solution wasn't just a memo from HR. Management implemented "resilience rotations," inserting two additional 15-minute breaks during the shift and bringing in temporary agency staff for the peak two hours of each night to alleviate the maximum pressure point. For the dispatch team, the issue was compounded by rigid start times that created a morning rush. By implementing a staggered start window of 5:00 AM to 6:30 AM, they reduced congestion and stress, leading to a 15% drop in absenteeism within two months.

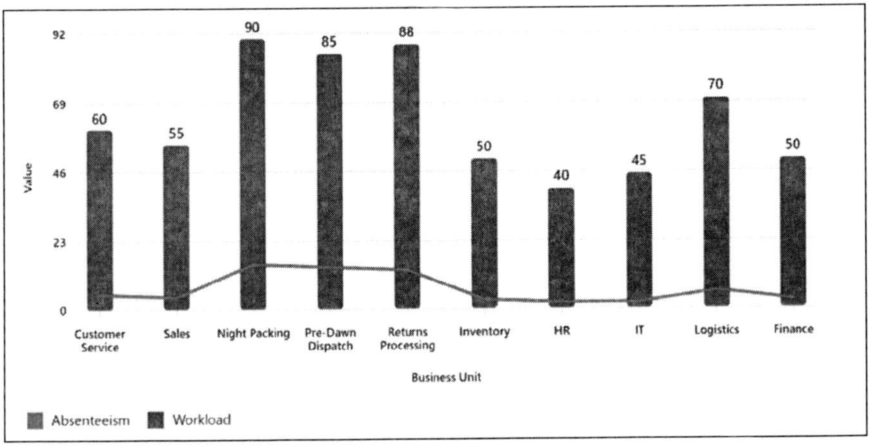

Graph 5.1: Workload vs. Absenteeism by Business Unit

This diagnostic step was guided by a simple but powerful question:

52. Which teams have the highest average absenteeism rates?
    – This highlights the units that are consistently understaffed, providing a clear prioritization list for managerial intervention. It moves the conversation from "we have an absenteeism problem" to "the night packing team is in crisis, and here is our action plan."

Mapping the Ripple Effect: The Hidden Power of Collaboration Networks

As absenteeism began to fall in targeted areas, ShiftWorks encountered a more subtle challenge: some roles, even with low individual absenteeism, could trigger massive disruption when they *were* absent. To understand this, they used organizational network analysis (ONA) software to map the digital communication flows between teams—emails, instant messages, and calendar invites—creating a visual Web of collaboration.

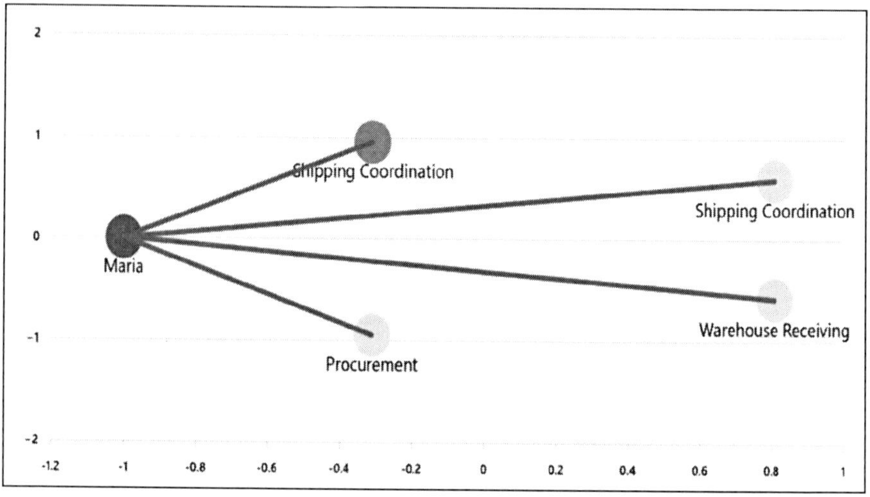

Graph 5.2: Collaboration Network – Maria's Operational Impact

The resulting network diagram was a thing of beauty and terror. It identified several "super-connector" roles. One was a senior inventory controller named Maria. Her node on the map lit up with connections to procurement, warehouse receiving, shipping coordination, and sales. When Maria was out for a week after a minor surgery, the entire system slowed down. Orders were delayed because no one else had her holistic knowledge or the trust of all the departments to resolve discrepancies quickly.

This understanding of operational vulnerability came from asking:

53. Which teams or functions collaborate most with others across business verticals?
    – This maps cross-functional dependencies and identifies the critical nodes in your workflow. These are not just employees; they are institutional linchpins. Their absence creates a ripple effect that paralyzes productivity far beyond their immediate team.

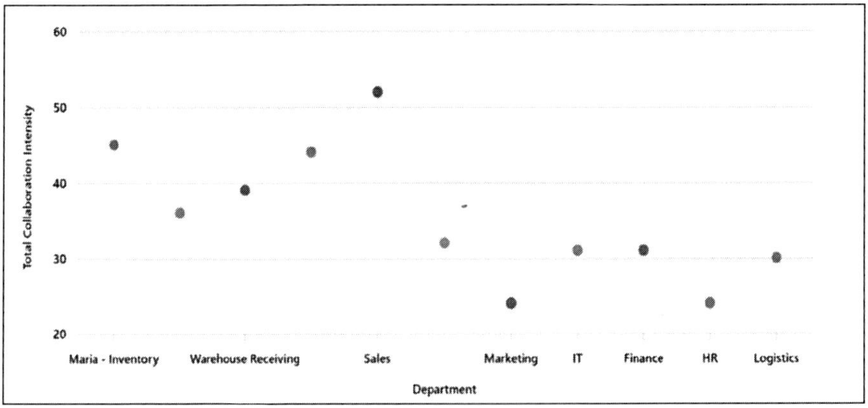

Graph 5.3: Strategic Connectors – Who Keeps the Workflow Flowing?

The strategic response was immediate. ShiftWorks instituted a "Cross-Training Crucible" program, mandating that every super-connector role must have at least one fully trained backup. This wasn't just shadowing; it involved a month-long rotation where the backup employee was empowered to make the same decisions as the primary. This built resilience directly into the organizational structure.

The Retention Solution: Flexibility as a Strategic Lever

Having diagnosed the problems of stress and single-point-of-failure risks, ShiftWorks turned to a more human-centric solution: rethinking the very nature of the shift schedule. The old model was rigid, drafted by managers with little employee input. The new approach was to pilot flexibility.

They launched "ShiftSwap," a self-service app that allowed employees to trade shifts with qualified peers, and "FlexBlocks," which let workers bid on compressed workweeks (e.g., three 12-hour days). The results were transformative. Departments that adopted these flexible models saw a 25% reduction in voluntary turnover. The most profound impact was, again, on the night shift. One employee, a single father, used ShiftSwap to adjust his schedule so he could take his daughter to school. "That little bit of control," he said, "made me feel like a person again, not just a cog in a machine." His turnover risk vanished.

This successful intervention was designed to answer a pivotal strategic question:

54. Do flexible work schedules improve retention in shift-based jobs? – This tests a critical hypothesis: that offering control and flexibility is a powerful lever to reduce turnover and maintain stable staffing levels in roles traditionally prone to high attrition. For ShiftWorks, the data confirmed that autonomy was more valuable than a minor pay increase for many employees.

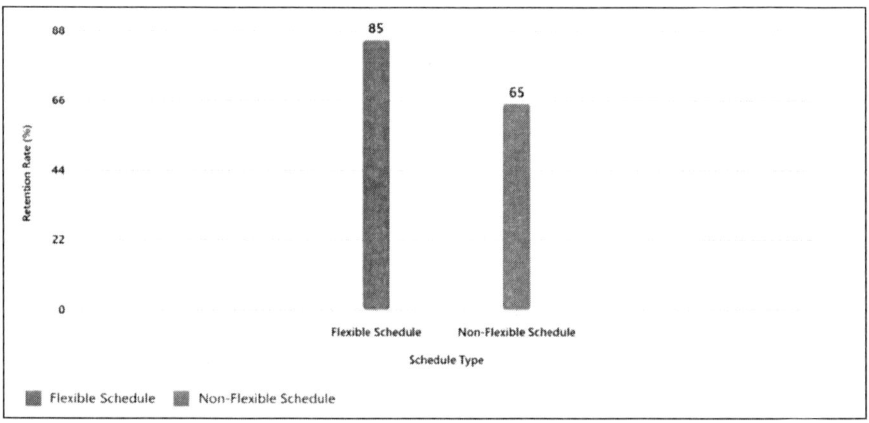

Graph 5.4: Retention Rates by Schedule Type – Impact of Flexibility in Shift-Based Jobs

Confronting the Inherent Challenge: The Night Shift Penalty

Even with newfound flexibility, the data confirmed a harsh, biological reality: the night shift was simply harder. A longitudinal analysis comparing day and night crews over two years showed that night-shift employees had a 40% higher baseline turnover rate. The line charts revealed predictable attrition spikes every January, as exhausted workers used the new year as a catalyst to find day jobs.

Accepting this inherent disadvantage meant that generic retention strategies were insufficient. ShiftWorks had to get specific. They implemented a "Night Shift Premium," increasing the differential pay. They introduced "Circadian Support," providing free healthy meal options and access to sleep specialists. Furthermore, they mandated a cap on consecutive night shifts and created a dedicated "Night Team Lead" role focused on morale and well-being, rather than just productivity.

To confront this inherent challenge head-on, they continuously monitored:

55. Do night shift employees have higher turnover than day shift employees?
– This assesses the specific retention impact of shift timing, validating the need for and ROI of targeted, more expensive interventions. It forces the organization to acknowledge that some parts of the workforce require a premium investment to maintain stability.

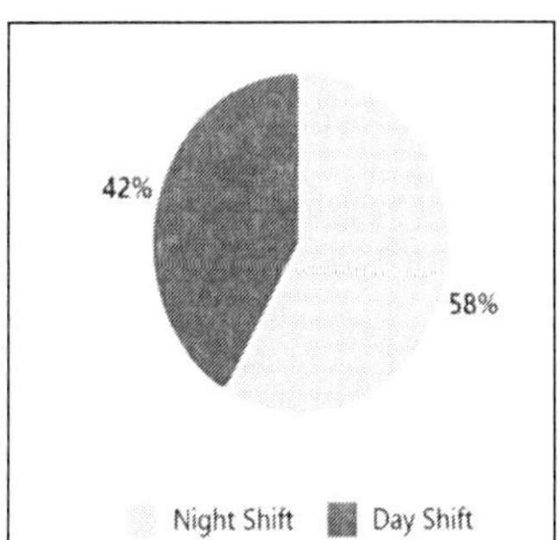

Graph 5.5: Turnover Distribution – Night vs Day Shift Employees

The Transformation: From Reactive Firefighting to Proactive Workforce Orchestration

By the end of the fiscal year, the culture at ShiftWorks had fundamentally shifted. The five core questions were no longer just an HR exercise; they were embedded in the daily dashboard of every operations manager.

- The **workload-absenteeism correlation** was monitored weekly, triggering automatic alerts to redistribute tasks before burnout set in.
- The **absenteeism heatmap** was reviewed monthly, allowing for proactive wellness checks and resource allocation to perennial trouble spots.
- The **collaboration network map** was updated quarterly, ensuring that cross-training kept pace with evolving workflows and newly emerging linchpin roles.
- The **impact of flexibility** on retention was a key metric for managerial bonuses, incentivizing them to embrace rather than resist schedule innovation.
- The **night shift turnover rate** was a standing agenda item in executive meetings, ensuring that the company›s most vulnerable employees were never forgotten.

The result was a more resilient, stable, and engaged workforce. Managers had evolved from schedulers to orchestrators, empowered with the data to make human-centric decisions that bolstered both well-being and productivity. Employees felt heard and respected, leading to a surge in positive sentiment on annual engagement surveys.

ShiftWorks' journey underscores a vital lesson: in the relentless, physical world of logistics and shift work, job structure and scheduling are the primary levers of operational health. They are not administrative tasks to be delegated and forgotten. By systematically asking these five questions, organizations can move from reacting to disruptions to proactively designing a workforce that is not only present but also productive, healthy, and loyal. In an industry where margins are thin and performance is non-negotiable, this strategic approach to the operational pulse isn't just an advantage—it's the difference between leading the market and falling behind.

Section 4: Key Takeaways

So, what did ShiftWorks teach us about job structure, shifts, and scheduling? If you think about it, this chapter was less about who was on the roster and more about how work rhythms, hours, and team connections affect the people who keep operations running. Here are the key lessons that stand out:

- **Workload matters as much as headcount** – High headcount doesn't guarantee productivity. Teams overloaded with work are more likely to call in sick, make mistakes, or burn out. Tracking workload alongside absenteeism helps pinpoint stress points before they become crises.
- **Absenteeism signals hidden risks** – When certain shifts or teams have repeated absences, it's more than just an HR metric—it's a sign that processes, scheduling, or morale may need adjustment. Addressing absenteeism proactively keeps operations smooth.
- **Collaboration strengthens resilience** – Teams that interact with multiple functions can better handle sudden absences or demand spikes. Mapping cross-team dependencies identifies critical nodes and informs staffing priorities.
- **Flexible scheduling improves retention** – Giving employees options to swap shifts, choose preferred hours, or compress schedules reduces turnover, especially for night shifts or high-pressure roles. Work-life balance is a tangible lever for workforce stability.

- **Shift patterns impact attrition** – Night shifts and extended hours consistently correlate with higher turnover. Rotating shifts, adding rest periods, and recognizing high-demand roles help retain talent.
- **Overtime is a warning sign** – Consistently long hours often precede absenteeism and mistakes. Monitoring overtime allows managers to redistribute tasks, hire temporary support, and prevent fatigue-driven problems.
- **Data-driven scheduling works** – Visualizing absenteeism, workload, and collaboration through charts and dashboards enables proactive decision-making rather than reactive firefighting.
- **Employee experience and operational efficiency are linked** – Fair rotations, predictable schedules, and cross-training aren't just perks—they directly affect productivity, engagement, and retention.

☞ **The bottom line:** Shifts and schedules are not administrative checklists—they are strategic levers. Monitoring workload, absenteeism, cross-team collaboration, and shift design ensures that the right people are in the right place, at the right time, performing at their best.

With these insights as a foundation, we now move to **Chapter 6: Hiring, Sourcing & Pipeline**, where the focus shifts from managing existing workforce rhythms to building and maintaining the talent pipeline needed for future growth.

CHAPTER 6

HIRING, SOURCING & PIPELINE

Section 1: Introduction

Hiring, sourcing, and pipeline management form the foundation of a resilient and future-ready workforce. Organizations can have strong internal structures, efficient shifts, and well-planned career paths—but without a consistent inflow of skilled talent, even the best-laid plans can stall. This chapter focuses on how companies attract, select, and onboard employees effectively while aligning talent acquisition with long-term business goals.

Think of the hiring process as filling a reservoir: the volume and quality of incoming candidates, the speed at which they progress through recruitment stages, and the channels through which they are sourced all determine whether the organization can operate at full capacity. Gaps or delays in this inflow directly impact productivity, project delivery, and overall workforce stability.

Beyond simply filling vacancies, modern hiring strategies aim to ensure quality, efficiency, and retention. Companies are increasingly leveraging employee referrals, diverse sourcing channels, and data-driven recruitment pipelines to attract candidates who not only fit current roles but are also poised to grow with the organization. Pipeline visibility, from application to onboarding, allows HR leaders to anticipate bottlenecks, improve candidate experience, and ensure that critical roles are filled on time.

Additionally, hiring is closely tied to cost management, business unit growth, and workforce planning. Recruiting the right talent efficiently can reduce turnover, stabilize headcount, and support both operational continuity and strategic expansion. An effective talent acquisition strategy balances immediate needs with long-term capability building, ensuring that organizations remain competitive in dynamic markets.

In this chapter, we will explore how companies can optimize hiring processes, manage sourcing channels, track recruitment pipelines, and evaluate the impact of various strategies on retention and performance. By understanding these dynamics, HR leaders can transform hiring from a reactive task into a proactive, strategic lever—keeping the organization agile, capable, and ready to meet future challenges.

Next, we will dive into **stories from the workforce**, showing how organizations navigate hiring complexities, streamline recruitment, and ensure a steady pipeline of capable talent to meet business demands.

Section 2: Data Sources

Before organizations can optimize hiring, sourcing, and pipeline management, it's essential to understand where recruitment and talent data comesfrom. Think of it like managing a river: to ensure a steady flow of water, you need to track the streams, tributaries, and dams. In talent acquisition, HR relies on multiple sources to see how candidates move through the pipeline, which channels yield the best hires, and how hiring affects overall headcount stability.

Applicant Tracking System (ATS)

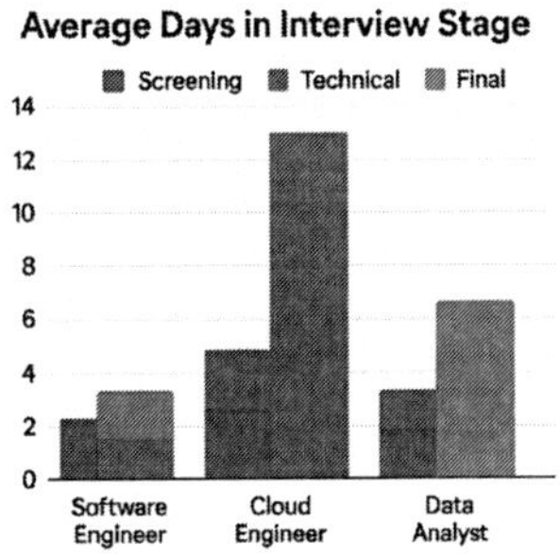

The ATS records every candidate's journey—from application to offer. It captures time spent at each stage, drop-off points, and eventual hires. This data helps pinpoint bottlenecks and inefficiencies in the recruitment process.

☞ Example: By analyzing average days spent in the interview stage, HR can identify which teams are slowing down hiring. For instance, TechNova noticed the technical interview stage for cloud engineers was taking twice as long as other roles, delaying new hire onboarding and impacting project timelines.

Human Resource Information System (HRIS)

HRIS provides the workforce context. Linking recruitment data to HRIS shows how new hires integrate into teams, affect headcount, and contribute to workforce stability. It also tracks internal moves and promotions, connecting hiring decisions with broader workforce planning.

☞ Example: HR used HRIS to track whether new cybersecurity hires were filling anticipated gaps. They discovered that although hiring targets were met, skill distribution was uneven across regional teams, highlighting the need for better workforce planning.

Employee Referral Programs

Referral data highlights which teams generate quality candidates and which sources yield hires that stay longer. Participation rates and referral success inform both pipeline strength and the efficiency of internal networks.

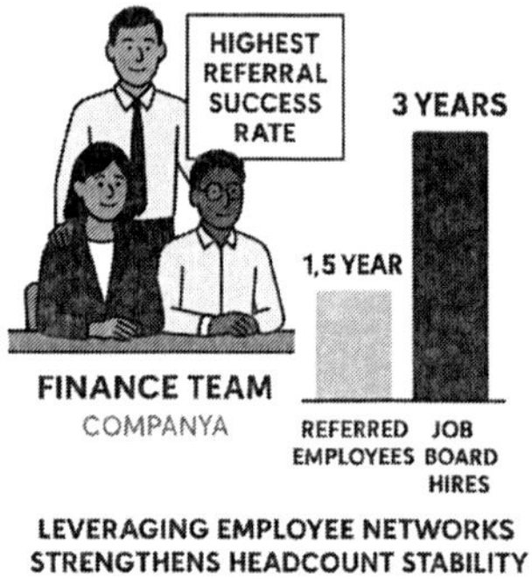

☞ Example: A finance team at BrightTech had the highest referral success rate. Employees referred by this team stayed an average of 3 years, compared to 1.5 years for job board hires, showing that leveraging employee networks strengthens headcount stability.

Hiring Source Analytics

Job boards, agencies, and other channels provide performance and tenure metrics. Understanding source effectiveness helps HR allocate budgets efficiently and anticipate where future talent will come from.

☞ Example: By analyzing hires from a coding bootcamp, HR realized these candidates had excellent initial performance but higher early attrition. The insight led to targeted onboarding programs to improve retention.

Market & Labor Data

External trends, like regional talent supply and skill availability, shape realistic hiring targets. This data helps HR anticipate shortages, surpluses, or market competition before it affects headcount.

☞ Example: When expanding in the southeast region, HR reviewed labor market reports and discovered a shortage of experienced data analysts. This prompted early outreach and tailored hiring campaigns to prevent gaps in operational capacity.

By combining these sources, organizations gain a 360-degree view of their hiring ecosystem. Connecting candidate flow, source effectiveness, and market insights allows HR to proactively manage pipelines, reduce delays, improve hire quality, and maintain stable workforce growth.

Section 3: The Talent Pipeline – From Chaotic Recruitment to Strategic Talent Cultivation

The Illusion of Growth: A Company Expanding and Eroding Simultaneously

TalentFlow stood as a darling of the tech sector, a mid-sized technology and IT services company whose growth trajectory was the envy of its competitors. For three consecutive years, the story told to investors and the market was one of unmitigated success, illustrated by a steep, unwavering climb in its headcount curve. Quarterly all-hands meetings were celebrations of new hires, with managers proudly displaying filled organizational charts. Yet, beneath the surface of this triumphant narrative, a deep and systemic crisis was festering.

In the trenches, the reality was starkly different. Project managers were in a constant state of anxiety, facing delayed product launches because key roles remained open for months. Team leads spent an inordinate amount of their time onboarding new members, only to see a disheartening number of them leave within the first year, taking their nascent knowledge with them. The finance department watched with alarm as the recruitment budget ballooned, with agency fees becoming a bloated and seemingly unshakeable line item. The company was, by all quantitative measures, growing. But qualitatively, it was bleeding—bleeding time, money, and institutional energy. TalentFlow was proficient at filling chairs, but it was failing catastrophically at building a stable, cohesive, and high-performing workforce. This churn was creating a hidden tax on innovation and productivity. A deep, diagnostic dive into their hiring, sourcing, and pipeline management was no longer a strategic initiative; it was an intervention critical for the company's long-term health.

The Untapped Goldmine: A Deep Dive into the Social Fabric of Hiring

The investigation began with the company's most touted but least understood asset: the employee referral program. It was a perennial bullet point in the HR team's presentation, a "strategic priority" that everyone praised but no one truly decoded. The first step was to move beyond vanity metrics—the total number of referrals—and into actionable intelligence. By mapping referral success rates (referrals that led to hires) against every department in the organization, a stark and telling divide emerged.

The data painted a clear picture: technical teams, particularly in software development and data engineering, were referral powerhouses. Over 40% of their hires came from internal recommendations. These teams were naturally leveraging their dense, active professional networks—forged through open-source contributions, conference attendance, and university alumni groups. The engineering culture at TalentFlow was one of collaboration and shared expertise, and this ethos extended seamlessly into talent sourcing.

In stark contrast, administrative, marketing, and operational teams had referral rates languishing in the low single digits. This wasn't just a participation gap; it was a cultural and structural chasm. These departments lacked the same ingrained, industry-specific networking culture. An administrative assistant's professional network was likely composed of other admins across various industries, not a concentrated pool of talent specifically suited for TalentFlow's needs.

The action taken was strategic. TalentFlow launched a "Referral Ambassador" program... This formalized and rewarded the behavior of their most effective talent scouts.

To further quantify the long-term value of this program, they added two more questions to their analysis:

56. How does referral program participation affect employee retention rates?
    – This examines whether employees who make referrals are also more likely to stay, measuring the program's impact on the retention of existing staff, not just new hires.
57. What percentage of referred hires are still with the company after two years?
    – This evaluates the ultimate success metric for referrals, moving beyond first-year retention to assess their true contribution to long-term workforce stability.

    This initial, critical discovery was guided by a foundational question about internal advocacy:
58. Are certain teams better at generating referrals than others?
    – This reveals which parts of your organization are actively co-building the workforce and which represent untapped potential. It highlights profound cultural and engagement disparities that can dictate the success of your talent acquisition strategy.

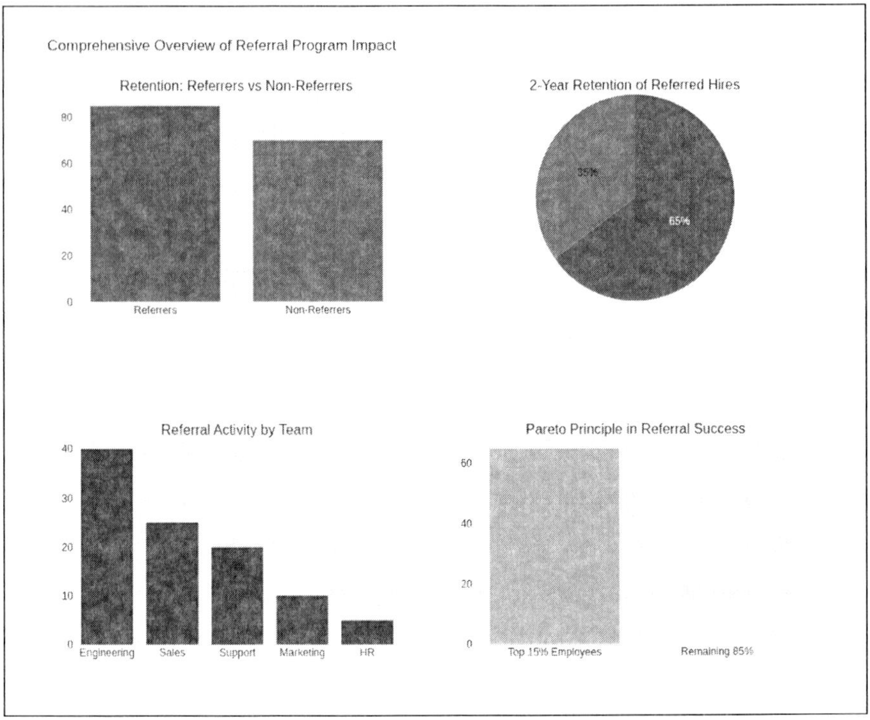

Graph 6.1: Comprehensive Overview of Referral Program Impact

Digging deeper, TalentFlow uncovered a fascinating Pareto principle at work. They found that only 15% of their total employee base was responsible for all successful referrals. However, this small, hyper-engaged cohort was incredibly effective, with a 60-70% success rate for their recommendations. This revealed the program's latent power: a highly engaged minority was already acting as an elite, pre-screening force, shortcutting traditional hiring barriers and bringing in candidates who were pre-vetted for both skill and cultural fit. The challenge was no longer just encouraging referrals; it was about understanding what motivated this 15% and replicating those conditions across the wider organization.

To quantify this engagement and its potential, they asked:

59. What percentage of our employees make a successful referral each year?
– This metric moves beyond vague participation numbers and highlights the concrete impact of a core group of employee advocates. It forces the organization to recognize that building a referral culture is about depth of engagement, not just breadth.

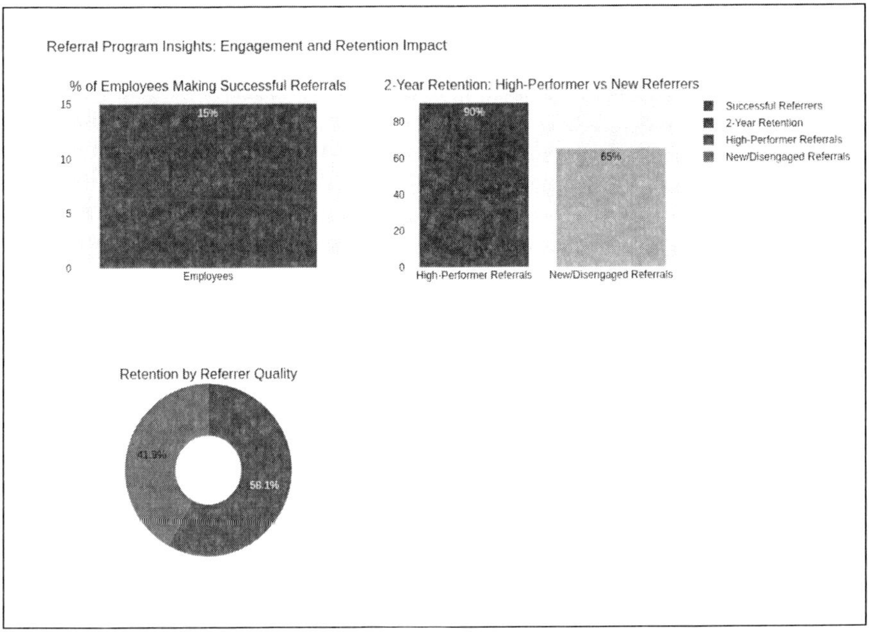

Graph 6.2: Referral Program Insights: Engagement and Retention Impact

The most profound revelation from the referral analysis came from dissecting longevity. A simple comparison of referral versus non-referral retention was positive, but the real insight was more nuanced. They discovered that hires referred by tenured, high-performing employees had a staggering 90% retention rate after two years. Conversely, referrals from employees who were themselves new or disengaged had retention rates no better than the company average. This wasn't just about finding candidates; it was about the quality of the social contract. A recommendation from a respected, long-term employee carried immense weight. It came with an implicit guarantee and a sense of accountability. The referrer provided a realistic job preview, acted as a mentor, and created an immediate sense of belonging for the new hire.

This led to two critical, strategic questions about the true value of referrals:

60. Do certain types of referrals result in better retention outcomes?
    – This examines the quality of the referral source, revealing that not all referrals are created equal. It shifts the strategy from "get more referrals" to "cultivate referrals from high-performing, established employees."
61. How does attrition for referred hires compare to non-referred hires?
    – This provides the overarching business case, demonstrating the referral program's direct contribution to workforce stability and its power to reduce the expensive, draining churn that plagues traditional hiring.

The action taken was strategic. TalentFlow launched a "Referral Ambassador" program, explicitly inviting their top-performing, tenured employees to participate. They provided them with clearer guidelines on sought-after skills and hosted informal "meet-the-team" sessions where ambassadors could bring potential candidates for a casual conversation. This formalized and rewarded the behavior of their most effective talent scouts.

The Clogged Artery: A Forensic Diagnosis of a Broken Recruitment Funnel

While referrals were a bright spot, the overall hiring engine was sputtering, failing to meet the demand created by aggressive growth targets. TalentFlow turned its attention to the recruitment funnel itself, treating it not as a simple process but as a dynamic system where time was the ultimate currency. A stage-by-stage time analysis revealed a critical, single point of failure: the technical assessment. What was designed as a swift, 3-day evaluation of coding skills was taking a paralyzing average of 14 days. The cause was a painful blend of high demand and limited supply. A mere handful of senior engineers, already burdened with critical project deliverables, were responsible for evaluating hundreds of coding challenges. Their "real work" consistently pushed candidate reviews down their priority list.

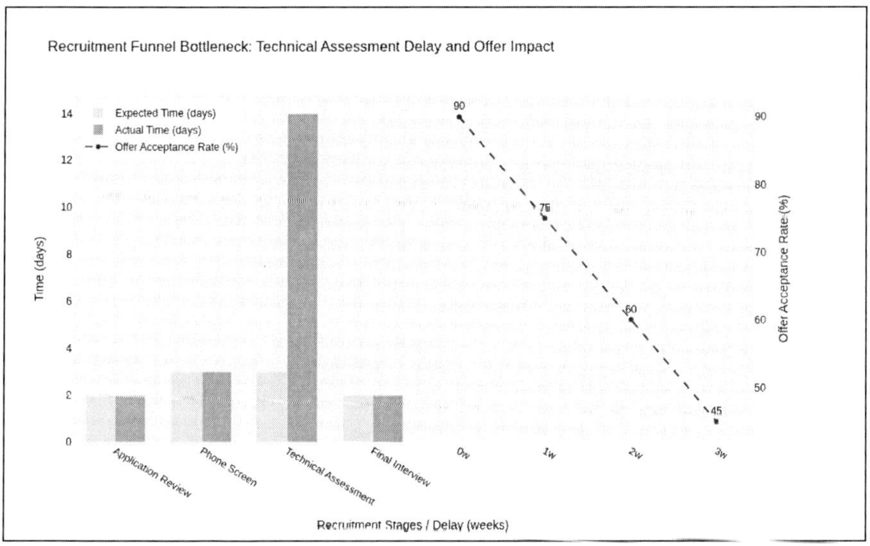

Graph 6.3: Recruitment Funnel Bottleneck: Technical Assessment Delay and Offer Impact

This delay was a silent killer of talent acquisition. In a competitive market for tech talent, top candidates are rarely on the market for long. They are often navigating multiple interview processes simultaneously. The data showed a direct correlation: for every week the process extended beyond the initial promise, the offer acceptance rate dropped by 15%. TalentFlow wasn't just being slow; it was systematically gifting its best candidates to more agile competitors.

Within three months of these changes, the average time from application to offer was reduced by 30%, and the candidate drop-off rate between screening and interview was halved.

However, TalentFlow knew that speed alone wasn't the only issue; they also needed to understand the causes of their delays and drop-offs. This led them to ask:

62. Is there a skill gap that extends time-to-hire for some positions?
    – This question moved beyond process to probe market reality. It helped them determine if slow hiring for roles like "Cloud Security Engineer" was due to internal inefficiency or an external scarcity of talent, requiring a different strategy altogether.
63. Which roles or teams have the highest average time-to-fill?
    – This pinpointed the specific positions (e.g., "Lead Data Scientist," "UX Research Manager") that were most damaging to project timelines, allowing for prioritized process redesign and specialized sourcing.

This critical, profit-draining bottleneck was identified by asking a simple but vital efficiency question:

64. Which step in our hiring pipeline is the slowest?
    – This pinpoints the specific stage where momentum dies and candidate interest wanes. It is the first step in targeted process

re-engineering, directly aimed at reducing time-to-fill and preventing the loss of premium talent.

The problem, however, was systemic, not isolated. A detailed funnel analysis revealed a staggering 60% drop-off rate between the initial positive phone screen and the first technical interview. This wasn't just a slowdown; it was a hemorrhage. Qualitative feedback from lost candidates cited a "black hole" feeling—a lack of communication, unclear next steps, and an overall impersonal experience. The company was spending significant money on sourcing to attract candidates into the top of the funnel, only to lose them through a fractured process.

To understand the scale and location of this leakage, they tracked:

65. What is the drop-off rate at each recruitment funnel stage?
    – This identifies the stages where candidate interest evaporates, providing a quantifiable measure of process inefficiency and its direct impact on headcount fulfillment.
66. Where in the pipeline do most candidates drop out?
    – This pinpoints the exact weak spots in the candidate journey, allowing for surgical interventions to plug the leaks and preserve the integrity and flow of the talent pipeline.

The solution implemented was multi-pronged and decisive. TalentFlow moved away from the "hero model" of relying on a few senior engineers. They created a "Distributed Reviewer Pool," training and certifying a group of 50 mid-level and senior engineers across different teams to conduct assessments. This not only diluted the burden but also sped up feedback times. They implemented a sophisticated automated scheduling tool (e.g., Calendly integrations) that eliminated the tedious back-and-forth emails to find a time. Most importantly, they introduced a transparent candidate portal where applicants could see their exact status in the process, view expected timelines, and access preparation materials.

Within three months of these changes, the average time from application to offer was reduced by 30%, and the candidate drop-off rate between screening and interview was halved.

The Source of Truth: A Rigorous ROI Analysis of Talent Channels

With the pipeline flowing more smoothly, TalentFlow confronted its most significant strategic blind spot: which sourcing channels delivered genuine, long-term return on investment? They began a rigorous project of correlating every new hire's source—be it referrals, specific job boards, agencies, or campus recruiting—with two key outcome metrics: their first-year performance ratings and their long-term tenure.

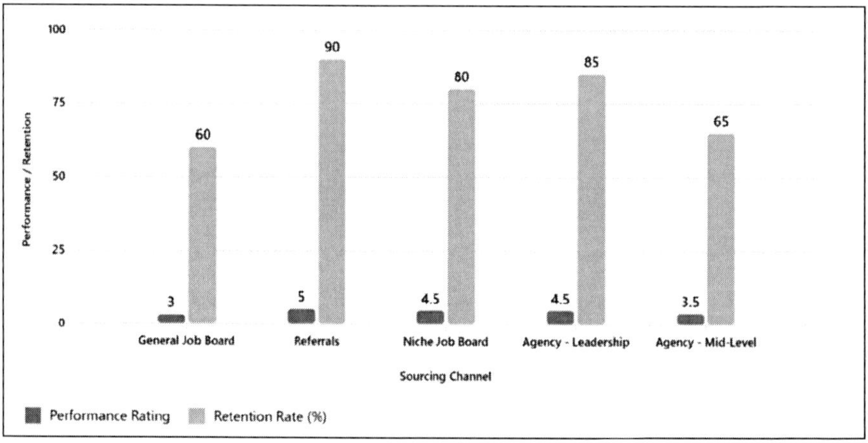

Graph 6.4: ROI Breakdown of Talent Sourcing Channels: Performance vs Retention

The results were transformative and, in some cases, shocking. While a major, expensive general-purpose job board delivered the highest volume of applicants, the hires from that source had middling performance scores and a devastating 40% attrition rate in the first year. They were filling seats with warm bodies who quickly became flight risks. In stark contrast, the low-cost referral hires were consistently top performers and showed the highest retention. Even more revealing was the performance of niche channels. Specialized job boards focused exclusively on developers yielded far better outcomes than general-purpose ones. Furthermore, agency hires for specialized leadership roles had strong retention and performance, while agency-hired mid-level developers often left within eighteen months, representing a significant financial loss.

The high cost, coupled with the high early attrition, meant the company was burning money.

To build a complete financial and strategic picture of their sourcing channels, they expanded their analysis with several critical questions:

67. Is there a correlation between cost-per-hire and tenure/retention?
– This was the crucial link between spending and value. They needed to know if cheaper hires were leaving faster (a false economy) or if their most expensive agency placements were actually justifying their cost with long-term service.
68. Which hiring sources are associated with the highest early attrition?
– This directly identified the channels that were creating the most instability and requiring constant re-hiring, allowing them to be deprioritized or fixed.
69. Is there a pattern of early attrition among hires from a specific channel?
– This nuanced question helped them distinguish between a generally bad channel and one that might be effective for certain roles but disastrous for others.
70. Which hiring channels correlate with the best long-term retention?
– This was the positive counterpart, identifying the champions of workforce stability to which they could allocate more resources.

71. Which recruitment source provides the largest share of hires?
    – This gave them a baseline understanding of their current dependency, revealing if they were over-reliant on a single, potentially risky channel.
72. Have our main sources of hire changed over the last three years?
    – This tracked the evolution of their strategy, showing whether their efforts to diversify sourcing (like the Referral Ambassador program) were actually shifting their talent mix.

This comprehensive channel analysis was driven by a series of performance-linked questions:

73. Which channels bring in hires who achieve the highest first-year performance ratings?
    – This determines which sourcing strategies genuinely deliver quality and capability, ensuring recruiting effort is aligned with building a high-performing organization, not just filling vacant positions.
74. Which hiring sources bring in the highest-performing new employees?
    – This reinforces and validates the link between source and performance, creating a virtuous cycle where the most effective channels receive more investment and attention.
75. Which job boards or agencies yield the longest tenure hires?
    – This connects sourcing decisions directly to long-term workforce stability, guiding investments toward channels that build lasting, committed teams, not transient occupants.

The financial implications of this analysis were equally stark. A straightforward calculation of cost-per-hire confirmed that agency placements were, on average, three times more expensive than referrals. However, the real story was in the nuanced calculation of Return on Investment (ROI). For some niche, hard-to-fill roles like a "Head of AI Ethics," the high agency cost was justified by the candidate's immediate impact and expected long tenure. For most volume roles, like "Full Stack Developer," it was a terrible investment. The high cost, coupled with the high early attrition, meant the company was burning money.

This led to the creation of a nuanced, tiered sourcing strategy:

- Tier 1 (Primary Channels): Employee Referrals and Niche Job Boards. These became the workhorses for 70% of all hiring, prioritized for their optimal balance of low cost, high quality, and strong retention.
- Tier 2 (Selective Channels): Specialized Agencies for leadership and hyper-specialized individual contributor roles. Their use was strictly governed by a business case requirement.
- Tier 3 (Sunset Channels): The expensive, low-performing general job boards were effectively retired, saving hundreds of thousands of dollars in annual subscription and advertising fees.

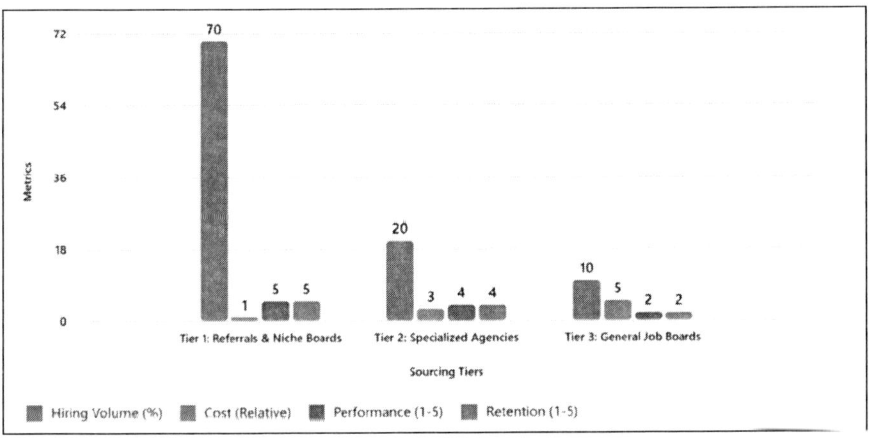

Graph 6.5: Tiered Sourcing Strategy Overview

This financial scrutiny was guided by critical ROI questions that moved beyond simple cost accounting:

76. Is the cost-per-hire lowest for internal referrals, job boards, or agencies?
    – This helps optimize the recruitment budget at a macro level, understanding the basic cost dynamics of different channels.
77. Have expensive hires yielded proportionately longer tenure?
    – This evaluates whether splurging on a candidate pays off in long-term stability, or if it is a wasteful indulgence that looks good on paper but fails in practice.
78. Which roles have the highest cost-per-hire with the lowest average retention?
    – This highlights the organization's most painful "revolving doors," signaling a critical misalignment in sourcing, selection, or even the fundamental role design that must be addressed holistically.

The Strategic Forecast: Aligning Talent Acquisition with Business Trajectory

The final piece of the puzzle involved shifting the recruitment function from a reactive service to a proactive strategic partner. This meant aligning hiring plans with the company's evolving business trajectory. TalentFlow began a rigorous analysis of growth vectors, asking not just "how many" but "who" and "what."

They discovered that their cloud engineering and AI services divisions were on a hyper-growth trajectory, projected to double in size over the next 18 months. Further analysis revealed that the most in-demand skills in these units were not just general programming prowess, but specific, advanced competencies in cloud-native architecture (e.g., Kubernetes, Docker) and machine learning operations (MLOps).

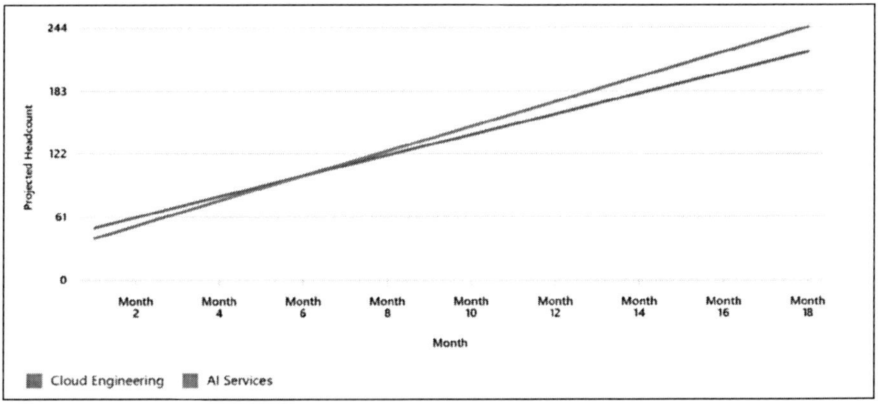

Graph 6.6: Strategic Hiring Forecast: Cloud & AI Growth Trajectory

This ensured they weren't competing for the same scarce candidates as every other company during the peak hiring seasons.

To fully transition from a reactive to a proactive function, TalentFlow's recruitment team began acting as internal strategists, asking forward-looking questions about trends, risks, and composition:

79. How do hiring trends differ by geographic region?
    – This revealed if their talent strategies needed to be localized, acknowledging that the candidate market in Austin was fundamentally different from that in Toronto.
80. When have we experienced unexpected hiring surges or lulls?
    – Analyzing past surprises helped them predict future ones, whether driven by a big client win, a product launch, or an economic downturn.
81. Which business units most frequently undergo hiring freezes?
    – This identified the parts of the business most vulnerable to economic shifts, prompting conversations about building more resilient, cross-trained teams in those areas.

82. Do our monthly/quarterly new hire numbers show seasonality?
   – This confirmed their intuition about Q1/Q4 surges, allowing for precise resource planning for their recruitment team and hiring managers.
83. What are the long-term patterns in our new hire numbers?
   – This macro-view showed them if they were in a period of sustained growth, stability, or contraction, directly impacting strategic workforce planning.
84. Have our diversity hiring targets improved over the last five years?
   – This moved diversity from a yearly snapshot to a trajectory, holding the company accountable for long-term progress and ensuring their future workforce would be more representative than their past.

This forward-looking, capability-centric planning was enabled by strategic questions:

85. What skills are most in demand in our fastest-growing units?
   – This ensures the recruitment team is proactively hunting for the right capabilities, preventing a catastrophic scenario where headcount targets are met with the wrong skillsets, creating capability gaps that throttle growth.
86. Which business units have grown the most in terms of headcount last year?
   – This provides a clear, data-backed picture of organizational expansion, allowing HR to proactively build sourcing strategies and talent pipelines to support ongoing growth rather than desperately react to it.

This analysis allowed them to build a "Skills Heat Map," which they used to guide university recruiting, tailor their messaging on job descriptions, and develop targeted upskilling programs for internal employees looking to transition into these high-growth areas.

They also began analyzing macro-hiring trends, discovering predictable seasonal surges in Q1 (post-bonus season) and Q4 (end-of-year budget spending). This allowed them to build a proactive recruiting calendar. Instead of waiting for a req to be approved, they began building "always-on" talent pipelines for critical roles, engaging with passive candidates months before the actual need arose. This ensured they weren't competing for the same scarce candidates as every other company during the peak hiring seasons.

The Transformation: Building a Sustainable Talent Engine

The journey TalentFlow undertook was not a quick fix; it was a fundamental rewiring of their approach to talent. By the end of their year-long initiative, the recruitment team had shed its identity as a reactive, order-taking function and emerged as a strategic partner armed with predictive data and a clear philosophy.

They had dismantled their inefficient, monolithic hiring process and replaced it with a dynamic, candidate-centric system. They had replaced costly, low-yield channels with a tiered sourcing strategy that maximized ROI. The once-crippling technical assessment bottleneck was now a streamlined, efficient process.

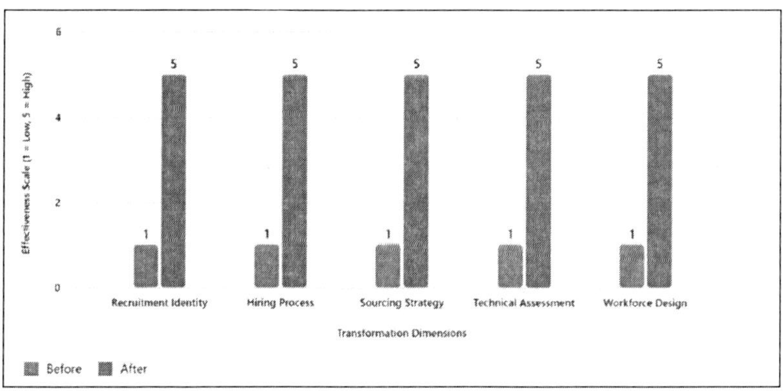

Graph 6.7: The Transformation, Building a Sustainable Talent Engine

Most importantly, they were now intentionally building a workforce designed to last and perform. By relentlessly focusing on channels and processes that delivered both high performance and long tenure, TalentFlow was simultaneously increasing its organizational capability and its operational stability. The rising headcount was no longer just a vanity metric on an investor slide; it was a testament to a sophisticated, data-driven talent cultivation system.

They learned that the true cost of a bad hire is not merely the recruitment fee; it is the compound cost of lost productivity, the drag on team morale, the time invested by managers in onboarding and offboarding, and the constant, draining cycle of having to refill the same seat. By asking the right questions—by treating talent acquisition as a science rather than an art—they turned their talent pipeline from a source of constant friction into a durable, sustainable competitive advantage. In the modern economy, where talent is the ultimate differentiator, TalentFlow has learned to build not just software, but a truly great company, one strategic hire at a time.

Section 4: Key Takeaways

So, what did the hiring, sourcing, and pipeline analysis teach us about building a future-ready workforce? This chapter was less about individual hires and more about understanding how talent flows, sourcing channels, and recruitment efficiency affect overall headcount stability. Here are the key lessons that stand out:

- **Referrals are a powerful lever** – Teams that actively generate referrals often contribute higher-quality candidates who stay longer. Tracking referral rates and success helps identify which teams drive the strongest talent pipelines.

- **Pipeline bottlenecks slow growth** – Hiring isn't just about sourcing; it's about moving candidates efficiently through the funnel. Identifying slow steps in the pipeline ensures headcount targets are met on time.
- **Source quality matters** – Not all hiring channels yield the same results. Internal referrals may cost less and perform better, while some agencies or job boards generate higher early attrition. Understanding which channels produce high-performing, long-tenured employees improves workforce stability.
- **Cost vs. retention requires balance** – Expensive hires don't always translate to longer tenure. Tracking cost-per-hire alongside retention and performance ensures recruitment budgets are used effectively.
- **Skill demand drives strategic hiring** – Fast-growing units require specific skills, and failing to identify gaps can delay projects or overburden existing staff. Aligning hiring priorities with skill requirements helps the organization scale effectively.
- **Geography and seasonality matter** – Hiring surges, lulls, and regional variations influence when and where headcount gaps appear. Anticipating these trends enables proactive planning and smoother onboarding.
- **Diversity and inclusion shape workforce composition** – Monitoring diversity hiring targets over time ensures the workforce reflects strategic values and supports long-term sustainability.
- **Data-driven recruitment strengthens outcomes** – Visualizing drop-offs, time-to-fill, cost-per-hire, and retention by source allows leaders to make informed decisions, reduce turnover, and maintain consistent headcount.

☞ **The bottom line:** Recruitment isn't just filling vacancies—it's about creating a steady, high-quality flow of talent that meets both current and future organizational needs. By analyzing referrals, sources, costs, pipeline stages, and trends, HR can optimize hiring decisions, reduce attrition risks, and ensure that headcount growth is strategic and sustainable.

With these insights as a foundation, we now move to **Chapter 7: Internal Movement and Attrition**, where the focus shifts from acquiring talent to managing and retaining it within the organization.

CHAPTER 7

INTERNAL MOVEMENT AND ATTRITION

Section 1: Introduction

Internal movement and attrition serve as vital indicators of organizational health and workforce stability. While recruitment addresses immediate staffing needs and promotions facilitate career growth, unplanned departures—especially following leadership transitions—can disrupt workflows, create knowledge gaps, and increase the workload on remaining team members. These disruptions often have ripple effects on productivity, employee engagement, and overall operational performance.

Understanding attrition patterns is crucial not only for filling vacancies but also for proactively managing workforce risks. Leadership changes, reorganizations, or team restructuring can trigger departures if employees feel uncertain about their career paths, reporting lines, or team dynamics. By analyzing historical data on departures, tenure, and internal movement, organizations can identify teams that are particularly sensitive to such changes and take preventive action.

This chapter emphasizes examining internal movement, focusing on how leadership transitions affect attrition rates and operational capacity. By tracking which teams experience the highest turnover after management changes, HR can prioritize interventions such as mentorship programs, clear communication of succession plans, and temporary leadership support.

Moreover, recognizing patterns in internal movement helps inform broader workforce planning and succession strategies. It enables organizations to anticipate potential skill gaps, allocate resources effectively, and maintain continuity in critical roles. Proactive monitoring also strengthens employee confidence, as staff feel supported during transitions rather than left to navigate uncertainty alone.

In essence, internal movement and attrition are not simply metrics to report—they are strategic signals. By understanding how shifts within teams, especially leadership changes, influence departures, organizations can maintain a stable workforce, enhance team resilience, and safeguard operational efficiency while supporting employee growth and engagement.

How might leadership changes in your organization impact employee morale, retention, and team performance, and what steps could be taken to minimize negative effects?

Section 2: Data Sources

Effective analysis of internal movement and attrition requires integrating information from multiple HR and operational systems. Together, these sources provide both quantitative and qualitative insights, helping organizations understand not just *who* is leaving, but *why* and *under what conditions.*

Human Resource Information System (HRIS)

The HRIS tracks employee tenure, role changes, promotions, and reporting structures. This foundational data helps HR monitor attrition patterns by department, tenure group, or leadership line.

☞ *Example:* If a team gains a new manager, HRIS data can reveal whether resignations increase in the six months following the change.

Time & Attendance Systems

Absenteeism patterns often serve as early warning signals for disengagement. By connecting attendance data with attrition trends, HR can spot stress points in teams facing leadership transitions.

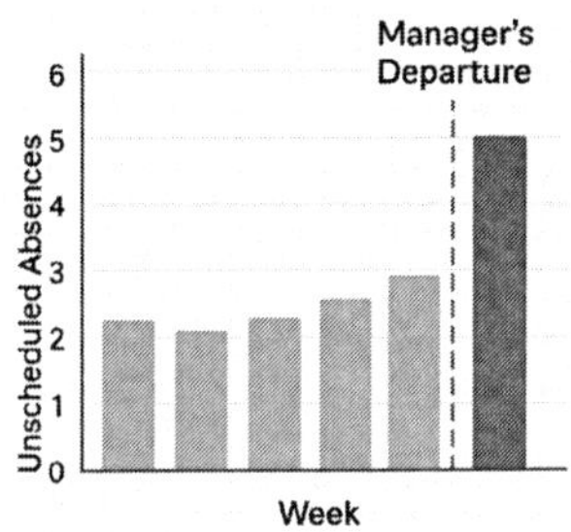

☞ *Example:* A spike in unscheduled absences after a manager's departure may indicate team strain before formal turnover begins.

Exit Interviews & Employee Surveys

These provide qualitative context, capturing reasons for leaving, perceptions of leadership, and levels of engagement. Surveys also highlight whether employees feel supported during internal transitions.

☞ *Example:* Feedback may show that employees resigned because they lacked guidance after a leadership change, flagging retention risks.

Performance & Talent Review Systems

Performance ratings, succession plans, and talent reviews identify critical employees and vulnerable teams. Linking performance with attrition uncovers whether high-value talent is disproportionately impacted.

☞ *Example:* If top performers consistently exit after a leadership shift, HR can intervene with targeted retention measures.

Collaboration & Team Interaction Data

Understanding how teams work together helps reveal where leadership changes might have the biggest ripple effect.

☞ *Example:* If a team relies heavily on a single leader for cross-functional coordination, their departure may cause noticeable productivity dips.

By combining these sources, HR gains a comprehensive view of how internal movement influences attrition and can proactively design strategies to preserve team stability and morale.

Section 3: The Ripple Effect: How Leadership Transitions Can Make or Break Your Talent Strategy

At InnoWave Solutions, a global software services firm, the quarterly HR report told a story of general stability. With over 4,000 employees, their overall attrition rate was enviable. But beneath this calm surface, a disturbing pattern was emerging—one that standard reports missed. Resignations weren't random; they were clustering, creating destabilizing waves that threatened critical projects. The common denominator? A change in leadership.

For years, employee departures had been treated as isolated incidents. However, when a revered senior project manager in the high-performing cloud engineering team left for a competitor, it wasn't an isolated event. It was the first domino. Within four months, six of his key team members had also resigned. The exit interviews revealed a consistent narrative: uncertainty about new reporting lines, fear that their hard-won career progression paths had vanished, and anxiety over who would champion their work with clients. The team wasn't just losing a manager; they were losing their navigator, and in the ensuing fog, they jumped ship.

This crisis forced InnoWave's HR team to move beyond counting heads and start diagnosing the ecosystem. They needed to understand if this was a one-off tragedy or a systemic risk.

The first, and most critical, question they had to answer was:

87. Does a leadership change in a team increase attrition within six months?

To find out, they created before-and-after line charts for every team that had experienced a leadership transition in the last two years. The data was unequivocal. In teams like cloud engineering and software architecture, the chart showed a flat line that spiked dramatically within 180 days of a manager's departure. This wasn't a coincidence; it was causation. The visualization transformed their understanding, proving that leadership turnover was a direct trigger for headcount loss and a very real threat to operational capacity. It was a leading indicator they had been ignoring.

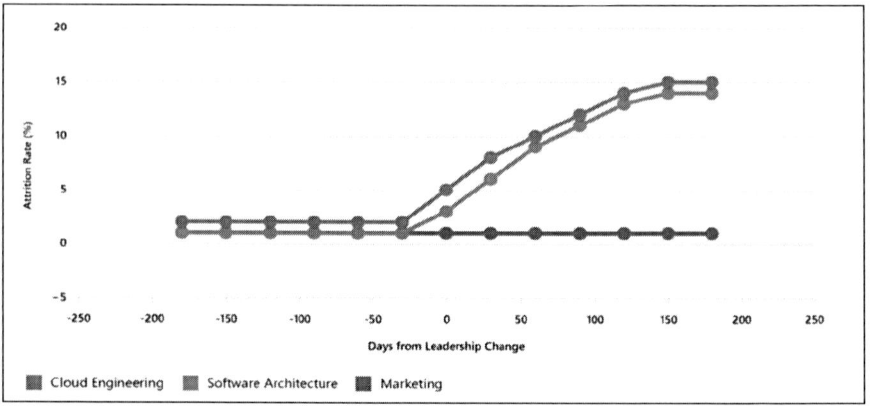

Graph 7.1: Leadership Transitions and Team Stability: Attrition Trends at InnoWave

However, the story wasn't uniformly bleak. In the same quarter the cloud team was unraveling, the marketing department also underwent a leadership change, yet experienced zero resignations. Why did one team fracture while the other remained intact? This contrast was the key to a more sophisticated strategy. It demonstrated that not all teams are created equal when it comes to managing transition.

This led to the next, more nuanced question:

88. Which teams are most sensitive to leadership turnover?

InnoWave created a visual heatmap of the organization, color-coding teams based on their attrition sensitivity following leadership changes. The pattern was clear. Teams that were highly technical, interdependent, and relied heavily on a manager for client liaison and technical direction—like cloud engineering and client delivery—glowed red with high sensitivity. These teams were like precision watches; disturbing the main gear caused the whole mechanism to falter.

In contrast, teams like marketing and HR, which were more autonomous and had flatter, more collaborative structures, remained a cool blue. Their work was less dependent on a single point of control, and their members were empowered with clear, distributed responsibilities. The heatmap was no longer just a report; it was a risk-assessment dashboard, allowing HR to anticipate trouble and allocate resources proactively.

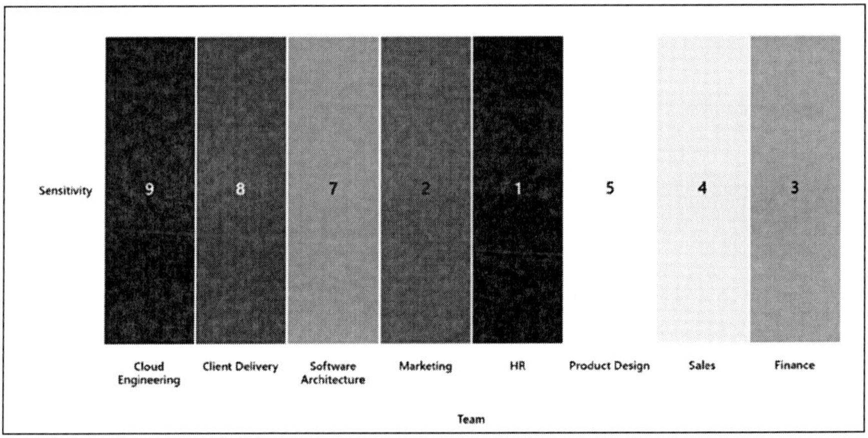

Graph 7.2: Leadership Turnover Sensitivity: Organizational Risk Map at Innowave

Armed with these insights, InnoWave moved from passive observation to active engineering of team resilience. They developed a "Leadership Transition Playbook" to be deployed preemptively in high-sensitivity teams. This wasn't a one-size-fits-all solution but a tailored set of interventions:

1. Interim Leadership & Succession Clarity: For any critical leadership vacancy, a qualified interim was named within 48 hours, and the timeline for a permanent hire was communicated transparently. This immediately quelled uncertainty about reporting lines.
2. Structured Mentor Pairings: Key team members were paired with mentors from other departments or senior leaders to ensure they had

a confidant and advocate beyond their direct management chain, safeguarding their sense of career progression.

3. Enhanced Communication Cadence: The first 90 days under new leadership were mapped with a strict communication schedule, including weekly team check-ins and one-on-one sessions to rebuild trust and align expectations.

The results were transformative. Over the following year, three other high-sensitivity units experienced leadership changes. By using the playbook, the attrition in these teams remained at or below the company baseline. The costly, destabilizing brain drain that had once seemed inevitable was now preventable.

InnoWave's experience underscores a critical lesson for modern organizations: attrition is not merely an HR metric to be reported on, but a cultural signal to be decoded. Leadership changes are inevitable, but talent loss is not. By asking the right questions—moving from "how many left?" to "why did they leave and where will it happen next?"—HR transforms from a historian of past departures into a strategist fortifying the future.

Ultimately, this proactive approach does more than preserve headcount; it builds a more resilient and trusting culture. It sends a powerful message to employees: "We are invested in your stability and success, even when your leader moves on." In doing so, organizations can ensure that leadership transitions become opportunities for renewal and growth, rather than catalysts for loss.

Section 4: Key Takeaways

So, what did our exploration of internal movement and attrition reveal about keeping organizations resilient through change? This chapter wasn't only about exits—it was about recognizing patterns of movement, understanding the ripple effects of leadership changes, and learning how to strengthen workforce continuity. Here are the core lessons that stand out:

- **Leadership changes ripple differently across teams** – Some units absorb leadership shifts smoothly, while others see a wave of resignations within months. Tracking attrition before and after manager changes helps identify where transitions pose the highest risk.
- **Team sensitivity matters** – Technical, interdependent teams often show higher vulnerability when a leader leaves, while more autonomous teams adapt better. Mapping team resilience through HRIS and surveys ensures interventions are targeted where they matter most.
- **Transparency reduces uncertainty** – Exit interviews repeatedly highlight that unclear reporting lines and career growth pathways accelerate departures after leadership transitions. Clear communication and succession planning help steady the ship.
- **Temporary leadership coverage prevents churn** – Leaving a leadership gap open fuels anxiety. Even short-term mentorship or interim leadership assignments provide stability during transitions.
- **Not all attrition is negative** – Internal movement, when intentional, can refresh career paths and unlock new opportunities. Distinguishing between regretted and non-regretted attrition ensures focus stays on retaining critical talent.
- **Data integration sharpens retention strategies** – Combining HRIS data, exit interviews, and pulse surveys creates a 360° view of why employees stay or leave, making interventions more precise.

☞ **The bottom line:** Internal movement and attrition aren't just about counting departures. They're about reading the signals, preparing for transitions, and building systems that keep the workforce steady even in moments of change. By tracking leadership impacts, identifying sensitive teams, and investing in communication and coverage, organizations can shift from reacting to exits toward proactively protecting headcount stability.

With these insights in place, we now move to **Chapter 8: Onboarding, Tenure, and Experience**, where the focus shifts from managing leadership transitions to understanding how new employees are welcomed, how long they stay, and how their overall journey shapes organizational success.

CHAPTER 8

ONBOARDING, TENURE, AND EXPERIENCE

Section 1: Introduction

Onboarding, tenure, and employee experience form the foundation of how organizations grow and sustain their workforce. Hiring brings in new talent, but it is the journey after day one that determines whether employees stay, thrive, and contribute meaningfully to organizational success. A well-structured onboarding program not only helps employees feel welcomed and integrated but also accelerates their path to competency. When employees reach productivity faster, teams achieve stability sooner, and the organization avoids costly cycles of re-hiring caused by early exits.

Tenure adds another dimension. Employees who remain with a company for the long term often provide continuity, institutional knowledge, and cultural depth. However, tenure without mobility can lead to stagnation, while rapid turnover creates volatility. The challenge for HR leaders lies in striking the right balance—retaining critical talent while ensuring growth opportunities keep employees engaged. Promotions, internal movements, and career development all intersect with tenure, shaping how employees perceive their future within the company.

At the same time, retirement and succession planning cannot be overlooked. As experienced employees approach the end of their careers, organizations must prepare for knowledge transfer and leadership continuity. A lack of planning here can result in "retirement cliffs," where multiple exits occur at once, leaving critical roles vacant and operations exposed.

By studying onboarding outcomes, tenure distribution, attrition by cohorts, and retirement risks, HR can identify where stability is strong and where vulnerabilities lie. More importantly, linking these insights together creates a holistic picture of workforce sustainability.

☞ The real question isn't just *how many employees join or leave*—it's whether the organization can help them ramp up quickly, retain them meaningfully, and plan for their eventual transitions in a way that strengthens overall resilience.

Section 2: Data Sources

Effective analysis of onboarding, tenure, and employee experience depends on integrating insights from diverse HR and operational systems. These sources provide both quantitative measures—like promotion rates, attrition curves, or onboarding speed—and qualitative perspectives that explain why employees stay, grow, or leave.

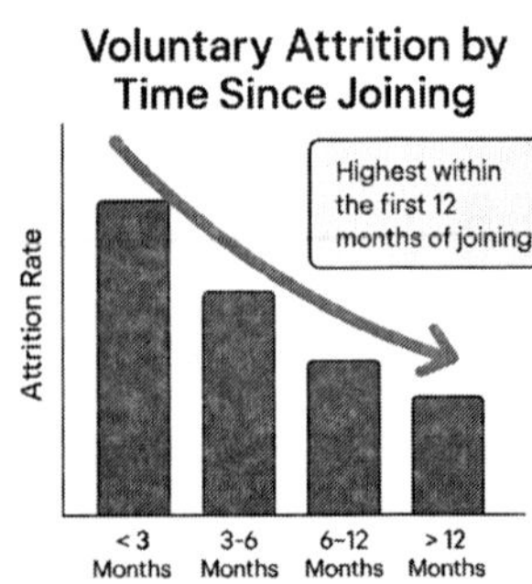

Human Resource Information System (HRIS)

The HRIS is the backbone for tenure data, role histories, promotions, and exits. It helps HR analyze patterns such as how long employees stay before their first promotion, or which business units show consistently high turnover among recent hires.

☞ *Example: HRIS can reveal that voluntary attrition is highest within the first 12 months of joining, signaling onboarding or role-fit challenges.*

Learning & Onboarding Platforms

Onboarding systems track completion rates, time-to-competency, and early training outcomes. This data shows how effectively employees ramp up and whether the onboarding pace correlates with long-term retention.

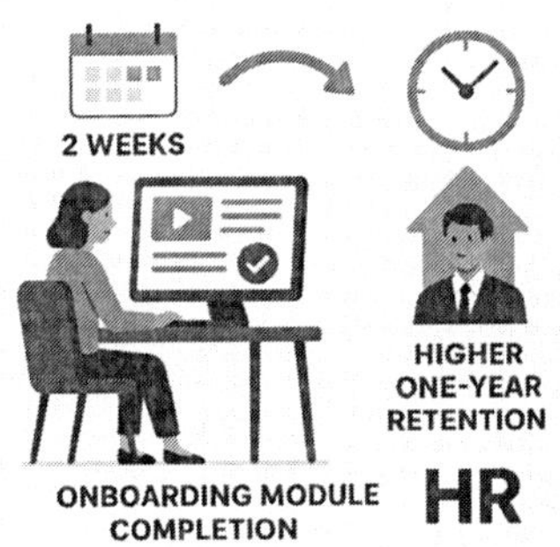

☞ *Example: If employees who complete onboarding modules within two weeks have higher one-year retention, HR can prioritize faster onboarding pathways.*

Performance & Talent Review Systems

These systems provide visibility into how tenure links with career progression and recognition. By combining promotion and performance data, HR can assess whether long-tenured employees are being developed or left stagnant.

If employees with more than five years of service show declining promotion rates, it may point to blocked career pipelines.

☞ *Example: If employees with more than five years of service show declining promotion rates, it may point to blocked career pipelines.*

Exit Interviews & Employee Surveys

Surveys and interviews capture experiences around onboarding satisfaction, growth opportunities, and retirement intentions. These qualitative insights explain the "why" behind attrition and tenure distribution.

☞ *Example: Surveys may reveal that employees left within six months because they felt unsupported during onboarding, highlighting design flaws in early-stage experience.*

Retirement & Workforce Planning Data

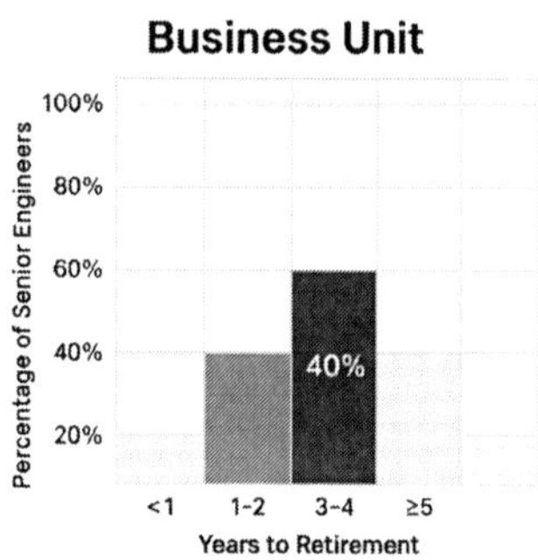

Age profiles, retirement eligibility, and succession plans provide forward-looking insights. They allow HR to predict retirement cliffs and identify roles without clear successors.

☞ *Example: A heatmap might show that 40% of senior engineers in a business unit are within three years of retirement, creating an urgent succession challenge.*

By connecting these sources, HR can build a holistic view of workforce stability—capturing how employees enter, grow, and eventually exit the organization—and design interventions that strengthen both individual experience and organizational resilience.

Section 3: The Employee Lifecycle Mirror: Building Stability from Onboarding to Retirement

At Orion Industries, a multinational engineering firm with 15,000 employees, leadership prided itself on stability and innovation. However, a deeper look revealed a workforce at a crossroads. The company was simultaneously grappling with disengaged long-tenured veterans, a revolving door of new hires, and a looming wave of retirements that threatened its knowledge base. The problem wasn't a single policy or manager; it was a disconnect across the entire employee lifecycle. To diagnose and heal these fractures, Orion had to move beyond simple headcounts and ask the right questions about the journey every employee takes.

The first crack in the foundation appeared in the company's promotion data. Veteran employees in manufacturing and field operations, the backbone of Orion for over a decade, felt increasingly overlooked. Their suspicions were confirmed by the data.

The critical question that exposed this growing inequity was:

89. How do promotion rates compare for long-tenured vs. recently hired staff?
    – A cohort comparison revealed a stark truth: newer hires in digital units were advancing faster, while long-tenured staff had plateaued. This wasn't just a fairness issue; it was a massive disengagement risk, silently eroding the loyalty of their most experienced personnel.

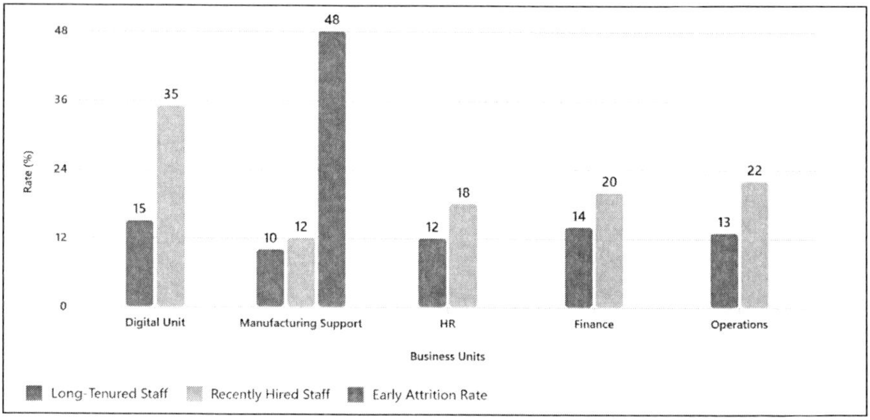

Graph 8.1: Promotion and Attrition Trends: Tenure-Based Inequities at Orion

Simultaneously, Orion was bleeding talent at the other end of the spectrum. In the manufacturing support division, nearly half of all new technicians were resigning within their first six months. This wasn't just attrition; it was a failure of integration.

To identify where this invaluable institutional knowledge was concentrated, they investigated:

92. Which business units have the highest average employee tenure?
    – A bar chart ranked by tenure confirmed R&D as a repository of deep expertise. However, this stability was a double-edged sword, masking a severe vulnerability.

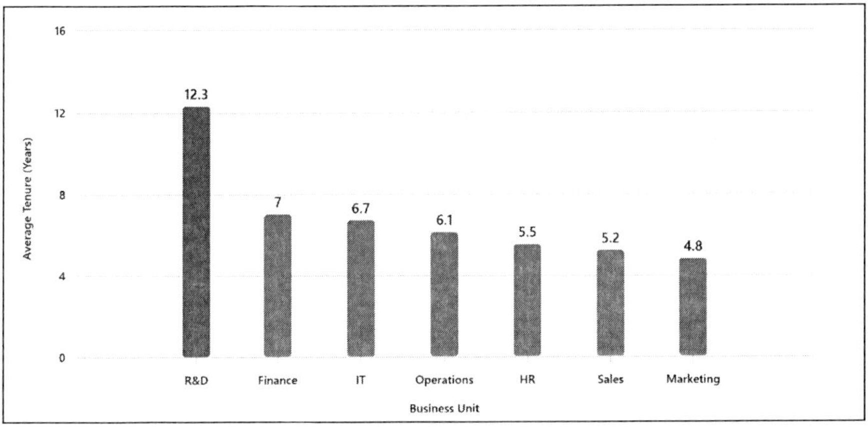

Graph 8.2: Average employee tenure across business units

Projections revealed that a significant portion of these senior scientists were nearing retirement age. Orion was facing a "retirement cliff" in its most innovative unit, risking the loss of decades of irreplaceable knowledge in fields like advanced robotics.

This looming crisis was uncovered by asking:

93. Where in the company is there a risk of a 'retirement cliff'?
    – Stacked bar graphs by age and function highlighted R&D and plant operations as high-risk zones.
94. How will projected retirements affect business continuity?
    – This forecasting question forced the leadership to look beyond the current headcount and confront the future talent gap.

The situation was even more dire when they assessed preparedness. A grim answer emerged to a pivotal question:

95. What percent of mission-critical roles lack clear successors?
    – The discovery that over 40% of critical roles had no identified successor was a wake-up call. The assumption that knowledge would be transferred organically was a dangerous gamble.

Orion's challenges were systemic, reflected in the fundamental health of its talent flow across departments.

96. Which teams have the most balanced ratio of promotions to exits?
– A scatter plot of this ratio revealed a stark divide. The digital transformation unit showed a healthy balance, fostering motivation. In contrast, the operations division was bleeding talent faster than it could promote, a clear signal of blocked career paths and deep-seated dissatisfaction.

The final piece of the puzzle was understanding the efficacy of their onboarding program. Analysis revealed that employees in customer service who underwent a rushed, two-week onboarding had significantly lower retention than those in a structured, phased program.

This proved the value of asking:

97. Do faster onboarding programs correlate with higher early retention?
– Regression analysis confirmed that speed sacrificed stability. Rushed onboarding led to confusion and early exits.
98. What is the average time to competency for new hires by role?
– Tracking this by role exposed major inefficiencies. While customer service hires were proficient in three months, compliance roles took nine, delaying their ability to contribute and frustrating both the new hires and their managers.

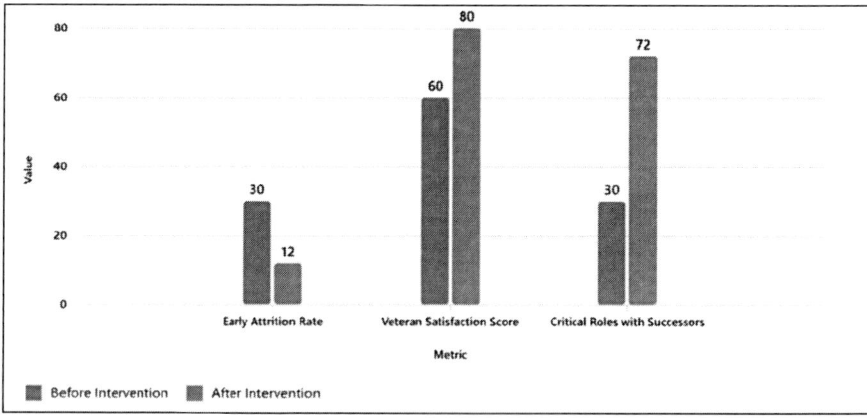

Graph 8.3: Impact of Strategic HR Interventions – Orion Workforce Transformation

Faced with this interconnected web of challenges, Orion launched a comprehensive counter-offensive. They redesigned promotion policies to ensure fairness for tenured employees while maintaining opportunities for new talent. They overhauled onboarding, replacing crash courses with standardized, mentorship-based programs. Most critically, they treated succession planning as a strategic imperative, identifying and developing successors for mission-critical roles and creating phased retirement and knowledge-transfer programs to avert the looming cliff.

The results were transformative. Within a year, early attrition dropped by 18%, veteran employee satisfaction scores rose, and a robust pipeline of successors was in place for over 70% of critical roles.

Orion's journey underscores a fundamental truth: workforce stability is not a matter of chance but of design. It requires proactively managing the entire employee lifecycle. By asking these essential questions, HR transformed from a reporter on past trends to an architect of future resilience. They learned that sustainable growth is built not just on hiring talent, but on nurturing it at every stage—ensuring that the organization remains engaged, capable, and ready for the future, from an employee's first day to their last.

Section 4: Key Takeaways

So, what did our deep dive into onboarding, tenure, and employee experience reveal about the invisible levers shaping workforce stability? This chapter was not only about how people enter and stay—it was about how organizations either accelerate success or silently set themselves up for costly turnover. Here are the core lessons that stand out:

- **Onboarding defines retention curves** – The first 90 days remain make-or-break. Structured onboarding consistently reduces early exits, while rushed or fragmented experiences drive higher churn within six months.
- **Tenure has two sides** – Long-tenured employees anchor organizational knowledge but can stagnate if not given growth pathways. Newer hires bring fresh energy but often face higher attrition if expectations and roles don't align quickly. Balancing these dynamics is key to sustaining capacity.
- **Not all business units age the same** – Certain functions like R&D thrive on long tenure, while others—like digital or customer-facing teams—require faster cycles of fresh talent. Recognizing these differences helps set realistic benchmarks for stability.
- **Retirement cliffs are predictable but preventable** – Clusters of employees nearing retirement create continuity risks. Workforce planning and succession mapping transform retirements from crises into well-orchestrated transitions.
- **Promotion-to-exit balance is a resilience signal** – Units where promotions outpace exits show higher engagement and stronger pipelines. Where exits dominate, it signals career bottlenecks or weak leadership.

- **Onboarding speed equals productivity speed** – Faster time-to-competency is a leading indicator of both employee confidence and long-term retention. Delays in training or unclear role expectations stall contribution and raise attrition risk.
- **Experience is the glue** – Surveys, exit interviews, and performance reviews consistently show that career clarity, recognition, and transparent communication are the biggest differentiators in whether employees stay or go.

☞ **The bottom line:** Onboarding, tenure, and experience are not isolated HR activities—they are the foundation of workforce resilience. Organizations that invest in structured welcomes, monitor tenure patterns, and design experiences that balance growth with stability don't just reduce attrition; they build a culture where employees see themselves thriving for the long run.

With these lessons in mind, we now move to **Chapter 9: Onboarding, Attrition and Experience**, where we explore how onboarding outcomes directly tie to attrition risks and how employee experience data can be used to predict—and prevent—early exits.

CHAPTER 9

ONBOARDING, ATTRITION, AND EXPERIENCE

Section 1: Introduction

Onboarding is more than a checklist—it is the first real experience employees have with an organization and sets the tone for engagement, productivity, and retention. While traditional metrics like time-to-fill or headcount capture recruitment outcomes, onboarding satisfaction and early experiences are leading indicators of whether new hires stay, thrive, or leave prematurely. Poorly structured onboarding not only increases early attrition but also undermines morale among peers, delays role competency, and impacts operational capacity.

This chapter focuses on exploring the link between onboarding satisfaction and early attrition, aiming to uncover which modules, activities, or processes most influence a new hire's decision to stay. By analyzing satisfaction scores, attrition trends, and correlations between onboarding experiences and early exits, HR leaders can pinpoint areas where improvements will have the greatest impact on workforce stability.

The questions explored here examine whether certain onboarding modules disproportionately contribute to early departures and whether low satisfaction scores serve as reliable predictors of attrition within the first months of employment. Understanding these patterns allows organizations to design targeted interventions, improve program effectiveness, and provide additional support where needed—ensuring new hires reach competency faster and feel integrated into the company culture.

By treating onboarding not as a one-time administrative task but as a strategic lever for retention, organizations can significantly reduce early attrition, accelerate productivity, and foster long-term engagement. This chapter highlights how data-driven insights from satisfaction surveys, attrition metrics, and onboarding analytics enable HR to continuously refine the process, making every onboarding experience a stepping stone toward stable, capable, and committed teams.

With these foundations in place, we now dive into **Section 2: Data Sources**, which outlines how HR collects, integrates, and interprets onboarding and attrition data to drive actionable insights.

Section 2: Data Sources

Analyzing onboarding, early attrition, and employee experience requires combining multiple HR and operational data sources. Each source contributes unique insights that help organizations understand not only whether new hires leave, but why and at which points in their journey they are most vulnerable.

Onboarding Feedback & Satisfaction Surveys

Surveys capture new hires' perceptions of onboarding modules, trainer effectiveness, clarity of role expectations, and organizational culture integration. High-resolution feedback highlights which modules are engaging, which are confusing, and which may contribute to early disengagement.

☞ Example: If the compliance module consistently receives low satisfaction scores, it may coincide with a spike in early attrition among those participants.

Human Resource Information System (HRIS)

HRIS tracks new hire start dates, role assignments, promotions, exits, and tenure. Linking onboarding participation with subsequent attrition allows HR to identify correlations between specific onboarding experiences and early departures.

☞ Example: HRIS data may reveal that hires in certain departments exit within three months of completing a specific onboarding track.

Time-to-Competency & Performance Systems

Performance evaluations and ramp-up metrics show how quickly new hires reach expected productivity levels. Delays in competency achievement often align with dissatisfaction or gaps in onboarding effectiveness.

☞ Example: A role requiring three months to reach full productivity may see early attrition if the onboarding program doesn't adequately prepare hires in the first few weeks.

Exit Interviews & Stay Interviews

Structured feedback from departing employees or those who recently completed onboarding provides qualitative context, highlighting unmet expectations, unclear role guidance, or cultural misalignment.

☞ Example: Employees leaving early may cite a lack of clarity in reporting structures or insufficient support during training modules.

By integrating these sources—surveys, HRIS, performance metrics, and interviews—organizations can create a comprehensive view of the onboarding journey, identifying risk points for early attrition, optimizing programs, and ensuring new hires become productive, engaged, and retained members of the workforce.

Section 3: The Onboarding Crucible: How BrightPath Solutions Turned Early Attrition into Long-Term Retention

At BrightPath Solutions, a thriving digital services company with 3,500 employees, success was measured by its ability to attract premier talent. The recruitment team consistently delivered impressive hiring numbers, bringing in skilled professionals from diverse backgrounds. However, this initial victory was quickly overshadowed by a troubling pattern: a significant number of these promising new hires were departing within their first six months. This revolving door was more than an HR metric—it was a direct threat to project delivery, team cohesion, and the company's hard-won reputation. The problem wasn't finding talent; it was keeping it. This realization forced BrightPath to scrutinize the very first experience new employees had with the organization: onboarding.

The investigation began by treating onboarding not as a monolithic event, but as a series of interconnected experiences. The company's program was comprehensive, spanning company orientation, role-specific training, compliance modules, and team integration exercises. To find the failure points, HR needed to move beyond general feedback and pinpoint exactly where new hires were disengaging.

The first critical question they posed was:

99. Are there onboarding modules where unhappy new hires are most likely to drop out?
    By mapping onboarding satisfaction scores against attrition data, a clear and troubling pattern emerged. The data visualized in heatmaps revealed a glaring hotspot: the mandatory compliance training module. While the content was essential, its delivery—a dense, monotonous e-learning course with minimal interaction—was causing widespread frustration. Survey comments described it as "disengaging," "overwhelming," and "disconnected from my role." Crucially, employees who reported low satisfaction in this specific module were statistically far more likely to resign within three months. This was a breakthrough. It proved that a single, poorly designed component could act as a catalyst for early departure, poisoning the entire onboarding experience.

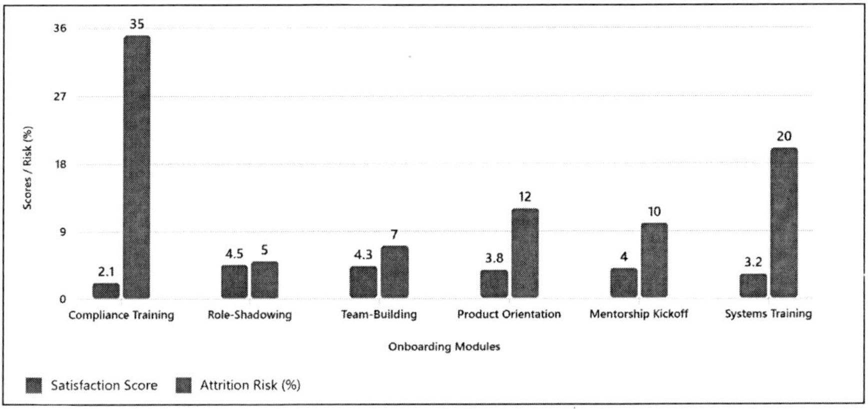

Graph 9.1: Onboarding Experience and Early Attrition Risk; Module-Level Insights at BrightPath

In contrast, modules that combined interactive learning with human connection—such as role-shadowing and team-building exercises—consistently received high marks and correlated with strong retention. This stark difference highlighted that onboarding effectiveness was not about the quantity of information, but the quality of the experience.

However, BrightPath needed to be more proactive. Waiting for employees to fail a module and then leave was too late. They needed a way to predict who was at risk.

This led them to their second pivotal question:

100. Does a low onboarding satisfaction score predict early attrition?
The answer, visualized through clear scatter plots, was an emphatic yes. The correlation between low overall satisfaction scores and subsequent departure was undeniable. New hires who felt unsupported, confused, or disengaged in their first weeks were signaling their intent to leave long before they submitted a resignation letter. This predictive relationship transformed HR's

role. They were no longer simply processing exits; they were now equipped to launch preemptive interventions.

The insights revealed that the issue was holistic. Exit interviews confirmed that early attrition was rarely about competence. It was a direct result of the onboarding experience failing to bridge the gap between recruitment promises and workplace reality. New hires cited confusion over reporting lines, ambiguous role expectations, and a feeling of being set adrift without adequate support. Even the most talented individuals struggled when the foundational onboarding structure was weak.

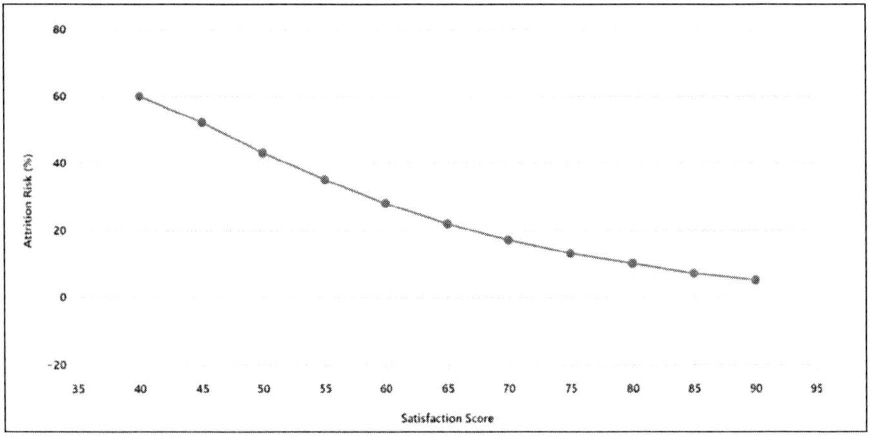

Graph 9.2: Predicting Early Attrition: The Impact of Onboarding Satisfaction at BrightPath

Armed with this data-driven clarity, BrightPath executed a strategic overhaul of its onboarding process. The problematic compliance module was broken into shorter, interactive segments with embedded quizzes and live Q&A sessions. More importantly, they institutionalized support, formalizing a 90-day mentorship program that paired every new hire with a seasoned colleague. Team leads were trained to conduct structured check-ins focused on clarity, expectations, and career pathing. To maintain a real-time pulse, they implemented weekly pulse surveys, creating an early-warning system to identify and support at-risk employees before they decided to leave.

The results were swift and significant. Within six months, early attrition plummeted by 40%. The heatmaps that once glowed with dissatisfaction now showed a much healthier, more engaged pattern. New hires were not only staying but were also reaching full competency faster, particularly in complex roles like technical project coordination and data analysis. This accelerated productivity directly boosted team capacity and project outcomes.

BrightPath's journey underscores a vital lesson for modern organizations: onboarding is the crucible where organizational loyalty is forged. It is far more than an administrative checklist; it is a strategic function that directly shapes retention and performance. By asking these two essential questions—where the experience breaks down and how to predict who is at risk—HR can transition from a reactive firefighter to a proactive architect of workforce stability. BrightPath learned that a deliberate, data-informed, and human-centric onboarding process isn't an expense; it is the foundational investment in a resilient, productive, and committed workforce.

Section 4: Key Takeaways

So, what did our deep dive into onboarding, tenure, and employee experience teach us about building a stable, productive workforce? This chapter wasn't just about welcoming new hires—it was about understanding how the onboarding journey shapes early retention, accelerates competency, and ultimately impacts headcount stability. Here are the core lessons that stand out:

- **Onboarding quality directly affects retention** – Employees who experience unclear, disengaging, or poorly structured onboarding modules are far more likely to leave early. By tracking satisfaction scores and correlating them with early attrition, HR can pinpoint which modules need redesign and which interventions will prevent turnover.

- **Early feedback is critical** – Continuous pulse surveys and check-ins during onboarding allow HR to identify at-risk hires before they exit. Real-time monitoring of satisfaction and engagement provides actionable signals to intervene and support employees promptly.
- **Mentorship and structured support reduce risk** – Pairing new hires with experienced team members, providing role clarity, and establishing check-ins builds confidence and accelerates integration. Teams that receive structured guidance demonstrate faster competency achievement and lower dropout rates.
- **Holistic experience matters** – Onboarding is not only about training content; it includes role clarity, access to resources, social integration, and understanding reporting lines. A well-rounded onboarding experience reduces uncertainty, builds trust, and encourages commitment.
- **Data-driven insights guide improvement** – Heatmaps of module satisfaction, scatter plots correlating scores with attrition, and time-to-competency metrics allow HR to prioritize interventions where they matter most. Data transforms onboarding from an administrative task into a strategic lever for workforce stability.
- **Early competency accelerates organizational impact** – Employees who ramp up faster contribute effectively to projects, improving team performance and reducing pressure on existing staff. Monitoring time-to-productivity highlights roles needing additional support and helps forecast resource requirements.
- **Predictive value of onboarding satisfaction** – Low satisfaction scores reliably predict early attrition, giving organizations a proactive tool to stabilize headcount and safeguard investments in recruitment.

☞ **The bottom line:** Onboarding is the foundation of employee experience and retention. By tracking satisfaction, providing mentorship, redesigning weak modules, and continuously monitoring progress, organizations can reduce early attrition, accelerate competency, and strengthen workforce stability.

With the completion of these 100 business questions of headcount theme, we now have a comprehensive understanding of how hiring, internal movement, tenure, and onboarding affect workforce stability. In the next volume, we will shift our focus to the **Engagement Theme**, exploring how employee motivation, satisfaction, and involvement drive performance and retention.

ANNEXURE

Some reports that organizations setup do serve as the firsthand data set to identify & track any of the trends:

Sl No	Report Name	Primary Audience	Key Insights & Combined Metrics
01WCD S001	**Enterprise Headcount & Diversity Snapshot**	CHRO, CEO, Executive Board	**A single-page, high-level overview.**
			• Total Headcount & FTE by Department/BU
			• Gender Diversity Ratio (% Female, % Male, % Non-binary)
			• Age Group Distribution (% Gen Z, Millennial, Gen X, Baby Boomer)
			• Key Trend: YoY Change in Overall Headcount and Diversity Metrics

Sl No	Report Name	Primary Audience	Key Insights & Combined Metrics
01WCD S002	**Talent Pipeline Health Dashboard**	Function Heads, VP of Talent, CHRO	**Analyzes the inflow and composition of talent.**
			• Hiring Trends: Experienced vs. Entry-Level Hires
			• Academic Background Diversity of New Hires
			• Diversity of Hire (Gender, Ethnicity)
			• Early Turnover (Attrition in first 12 months)
01WCD S003	**Leadership & Succession Readiness Report**	CHRO, CEO, Board, DEI Council	**Focuses on current and future leadership health.**
			• Gender & Diversity Representation at Each Job Level (especially leadership)
			• Age & Retirement Risk Analysis for critical roles
			• Internal Promotion Rate & Trends
			• Succession Pipeline Coverage for key positions

Sl No	Report Name	Primary Audience	Key Insights & Combined Metrics
01WCD S004	**Organizational Structure & Role Analysis, Skill Gap Analysis**	Function Heads, COO, HRBPs	**Examines the balance and efficiency of team structures.**
			• Role Concentration (e.g., # of Developers vs. Testers)
			• Span of Control (Manager-to-Employee Ratios)
			• Department-wise Headcount Distribution
			• Hierarchical Layers by Business Unit
01WCD S005	**Geographic Distribution & Strategy Map**	COO, Regional Heads, CHRO	**Visualizes workforce location strategy and risks.**
			• Headcount Distribution by Region/Country/City
			• Role Variety by Location (e.g., HQ vs. Satellite offices)
			• Gender Balance by Geography
			• Identify Growth Hotspots & Support Gaps

Sl No	Report Name	Primary Audience	Key Insights & Combined Metrics
01WCD S006	**DEI Deep Dive: Representation & Equity**	DEI Council, CHRO, All Function Heads	**A detailed look at equity across the entire organization.**
			• Detailed Gender Split by Level, Department, and Location
			• Pay Equity Indicators (by level and function)
			• Promotion Rate by Demographic Group
			• Inclusion & Belonging Survey Scores (if available)
01WCD S007	**Workforce Composition Trends & Forecast**	CHRO, CEO, Strategy Team	**Tracks changes over time and projects future composition.**
			• Multi-Year Trends in Age, Gender, and Tenure Distribution
			• Forecasted Retirement & Attrition Risks
			• Projected Headcount Growth by Department/ Location
			• Benchmarking vs. Industry Diversity Standards

ENDNOTE

"As I look back on this journey, I realize that when I first began this research, I never imagined it would one day become a book. I was simply exploring patterns, validating hypotheses, and making sense of workforce data. With my background in statistics and actuarial science, I've always believed that analysis must be understandable even to those without an analytical mindset—and that belief shaped every page.

This book is built entirely on original datasets and proprietary analysis from Talent Synergy Solutions, the result of nearly 18,000 hours of research and discovery conducted between 2023 and 2025. I hope this work opens a fresh perspective on the HR Analytics journey—one that encourages readers to think differently, explore deeper, and see beyond the numbers. At the same time, we hope HR practitioners to make use of the correlation of the business problems through the data visualizations and be more hands-on in their data/storytelling journey.

My wish is that you continue walking with us uncovering new ways of understanding the people and stories behind the data."

– Prarthana Karmakar (Author)

Reach me: https://www.linkedin.com/in/prarthana123/